The Region Beyond

The Region Beyond

From the Land Down Under

BARRY BLACKSTONE

RESOURCE *Publications* • Eugene, Oregon

THE REGION BEYOND
From the Land Down Under

Copyright © 2012 Barry Blackstone. All rights reserved. Except for brief quotations in critical publications or reviews, no part of this book may be reproduced in any manner without prior written permission from the publisher. Write: Permissions, Wipf and Stock Publishers, 199 W. 8th Ave., Suite 3, Eugene, OR 97401.

Resource Publications
An Imprint of Wipf and Stock Publishers
199 W. 8th Ave., Suite 3
Eugene, OR 97401

www.wipfandstock.com

ISBN 13: 978-1-62032-112-6

Manufactured in the U.S.A.

To my dear cousin, Bob, on this the 40th anniversary of our pioneer short-term mission's trip into the outback of Australia.

Contents

Prelude • ix
Introduction—The Region Beyond • xiii

1. The Land Down Under • 1
2. God Gives another Aaron • 4
3. Where in Australia to Go? • 6
4. But My God Shall Supply • 8
5. Thirty-One Dollars and Fifty Cents • 10
6. The Day of Departure • 12
7. Walking by Faith and Not by Sight • 15
8. There is a Friend • 17
9. The Marathon across America • 19
10. A Threefold Cord is Not Quickly Broken • 22
11. A Short Stay in Eden • 24
12. The One Ocean Concept • 26
13. Pacific Revelation • 28
14. Australia Island • 31
15. The Evening and the Morning were the First Day • 33
16. Greater Love Hath No Man than This • 35
17. Starts and Stops • 37
18. Stranded in Melbourne • 39
19. Melbourne Ministries • 41
20. Go West, Young Man, Go West • 43

21	Straight and Narrow •	45
22	Anticipation •	47
23	Kalgoorlie •	49
24	A Wilderness, a Dry Land, a Desert •	51
25	Something New •	53
26	Cosmo Newbery •	55
27	Moving On •	57
28	The Southern Cross •	60
29	Warburton Range Mission •	62
30	Answer to Prayer •	64
31	Gibson Desert Aborigines •	66
32	Two are better than one •	68
33	Feed My Lambs •	70
34	Whatsoever Ye Do •	72
35	One •	74
36	Blackstone •	77
37	The Word of God •	79
38	Rendezvous in Warburton •	82
39	They Returned Again •	84
40	Cold Water •	86
41	Apollo's Watered •	88
42	Spiritual Adversaries •	90
43	Trouble at Warburton •	92
44	A Strange People of a Strange Land •	94
45	Goodbye to the Gibson Desert •	97
46	Detour •	99
47	From Mount Margret to Cundeelee •	101
48	Life's Railway to Heaven •	103
49	Walter F. Betts •	105
50	The Statue of Liberty •	107
	Postlude • 109	

Prelude

I Thessalonians 5:24: "Faithful is he that calleth you, who also will do it."

I HAVE HAD 40 years to reflect on the greatest spiritual adventure of my life: a summer spent as a short-term missionary in the Gibson Desert of Western Australia serving with the United Aborigines Mission, ministering among an Aboriginal tribe in an out-of-the-way place called Warburton.

As I grow older and my memories fade, I am determined to leave my spiritual observations to those that follow behind. I have written about many personal experiences in my pilgrimage to heaven, but this special 10-week period of my early life I have kept to myself all these years. The trip to Warburton Range Mission Station (In 1972, this was the remotest mission station in the world, 300 miles north, south, east, or west from any settlement of any kind.) is not unknown to my family or closest friends, but what happened at that mission station has remained a secret of my heart to this day. It was there the Lord redirected my steps, and in truth, the rest of my life. (Just three short weeks from now, I will have completed 39 years in the pastorate!) If I hadn't taken 'the road less traveled'—the life of a local pastor in a small place— I wouldn't have married my wife Coleen, brought into this world my son, Scott (a specialist in the United States Army), and my daughter, Marnie (who at the writing of these observation is in her final year at Dallas Theological Seminary having repeated my Australia experience in Africa, India, and Europe), or pastored four local churches, each a unique part of Christ's body.

Prelude

It wasn't until many years later that my disappointment of not being called to a missionary's ministry was finally answered when the Lord spoke through these verses in Ezekiel:

"And he said unto me, Son of man (Barry Blackstone), go, get thee unto the house of Israel (my own people of New England), and speak with my words (the Bible) unto them. For thou art not sent to a people of a strange speech (Here is the first line of 'Away in a Manger' in the language of the Aborigines of Warburton: 'Pulukangka yitingka, ngura wiyangka; Mitilypa Tjiitjanya Puurpa ngariingu.') and of a hard language (Here is the second line of that Christmas carol: 'Pintiri pinilu kaninytjara nyangu Puurpa Tyiitjanya kunkunpa ngaringu.'), but to the house of Israel (my own people of Maine); not to many people (I have only pastored small, out-of-the-way churches of a few people.) of a strange speech (Wongi) and of a hard language (of the Western Desert Aborigines of Australia), whose words thou canst not understand. Surely, had I sent thee to them, they would have hearkened unto thee (promised success and an open ear). But the house of Israel (my own people of Aroostook County) will not hearken unto thee (In 1986, I was rejected by my home church to be their pastor, a ministry I felt called to.); for they will not hearken unto me: for all the house of Israel are impudent and hardhearted." (Ezekiel 3:4–7)

In 1972, I had a missionary's heart, but I never got a missionary's calling. From the time I boarded a small plane in Presque Isle, Maine, on June 7, 1972, until I returned home to Perham, Maine, 68 days later, the Lord God went about His business of reshaping and remodeling my spiritual journey and my pastor's heart. Little did I know of the disappointments that awaited me as my heart's desire was rejected and I clearly heard the word 'No' on that dusty plain of Warburton? Perhaps, Charles A. Tindley put it best in his classic church hymn, "We'll Understand it Better By and By." His words have spoken volumes to me:

> "Trials dark on every hand, and we cannot understand all
> the ways that God would lead us to that blessed Promised

Prelude

Land; but He'll guide us with His eye, and we'll follow till we die; we will understand it better by and by. Oft our cherished plans have failed, disappointments have prevailed, and we've wandered in the darkness, heavy-hearted and alone; but we're trusting in the Lord and, according to His Word, we will understand it better by and by. Temptations, hidden snares often take us unawares, and our hearts are made to bleed for some thoughtless word or deed, and we wonder why the test, when we try to do our best, but we'll understand it better by and by. By and by, when the morning comes, when the saints of God are gathered home, we will tell the story how we've overcome; we will understand it better by and by."

This is my story! Is not this the concept Jesus shared with his dear disciple Peter on the night of his most difficult crossroad? "Jesus answered and said unto him, What I do thou knowest not now; but thou shalt know hereafter" (John 13:7). It is a concept I am still learning as I share with you the insights I experienced during that special summer of '72. My prayer is that you, like me, will learn the precept printed at the beginning of this prelude. Paul's verse to the Church of Thessalonica was my special promise for that special summer, and all the summers since. Despite the fact that I never returned to Australia, God's "exceeding great and precious" (II Peter 1:4) promises sustained me and still sustains me. I understand now that God does know best, even when our heart desires something else. I was surprised by God's redirection, but I learned to accept it. May these stories help you to do the same when 'the region beyond' is not for you!

—Barry Blackstone
June 7, 1972

Introduction

II CORINTHIANS 10:16-To preach the Gospel in **the regions beyond** you and not to boast in another man's line of things made ready to our hand.

ONE OF THE ADVANTAGES of writing the history of a period in one's life forty years later is the ability to fill in some of details that were unknown to you four decades earlier. Little did I know in 1972 that I would make several more trips into 'the regions beyond', not in Australia, but in India? In 2006 I made my first trip (I have made two more at the writing of this book) to the subcontinent of Asia and found that my hunger-lust for the great 'beyond' was still beating in my heart. It was at a small Bible College in Kerala State that I met a generation of young people with the same desire to reach the unreached that I had when I was in college. It was there I heard them sing for the first time A. B. Simpson's classic missionary hymn based on Paul's desire printed above. Margaret, his wife, wrote the melody, and the title was taken directly from Paul's verse:

THE REGIONS BEYOND

> "To the regions beyond I must go, I must go, where the story has never been told; to the millions that never have heard of His love, I must tell the sweet story of old. To the hardest of places He calls me to go, not thinking of comfort or ease; the world may pronounce me a dreamer, a fool, enough if the Master I please. Oh, ye that are spending your leisure and powers in pleasures so foolish and

fond; awake from your selfishness, folly and sin, and go to the regions beyond. There are other 'lost sheep' that the Master must bring, and they must the message be told; He sends me to gather them out of all lands, and welcome them back to His fold. To the regions beyond, I must go, I must go, till the world, all the world, His salvation shall know."

Despite being a country pastor for most of my adult life in New England, I did periodically wandered to far-off and distant places that kept this desire alive. In 1975, just two years into my first pastorate, I was off to the back-country of Northern Quebec, Canada with a group of young men as camp pastor of a Boy's Brigade ministry out of Maine. Since that first trip to the beyond regions of Canada, I have returned to America's neighbor to the north nearly two dozen times to 'preach the Gospel'. But it was when I walked through an open door into the fabled land of India that "Australia feeling" of really going to 'the regions beyond' returned. In my last trip in 2010, I was able to repeat a 'train-trip' I had first experienced in Australia, and reach into the outback of the State of Andrah Pardesh. Traveling through similar desert country, I was determined to return and write of my experiences, and I have in a book I call "From Venmony to Kanekel and Between", the last of a trilogy of books on other far-a-field adventures I have had in my life (the other two books are "From Maine to India and Back"-my first two trip to India and "From Dan to Beersheba and Beyond"-my three weeks traveling around Israel in 2010).

When I got back from these spiritual adventures I felt that it was important to get out my old journal from my Australia trip and relive the experiences I shared with my cousin Bob, and be reminded what the Lord did that summer to shape the rest of my ministry life. One year after I returned from Australia I started serving my Lord and Saviour in the out-of-the-way places of New England; first in the small New Hampshire village of Pembroke, then in the even smaller farming community of Westfield

Introduction

in Aroostook County, Maine, then on an island (Moose Island) off the downeast coast of Maine, and now in the coastal city of Ellsworth in central Maine. To some, I have gone in my entire pastorate life to 'the regions beyond'. I still recall an encounter I had on my very first Sunday as pastor of the Emmanuel Baptist Church in Ellsworth. I was nervous about starting my very first 'city-pastorate', and asked the congregation to pray for me during my first sermon. After the service two tall men asked if they might speak with me. Because I didn't know the difference between parishioners and visitors, I imagined the worst thinking I had already made some kind of mistake. The men started out by saying they wanted to debate with me my use of the term 'city'. At first I couldn't understand what they could be talking about: 'city'? It was then they introduced themselves to me as being two visitors from Hartford, Connecticut and that our little city of Ellsworth would only be considered a hamlet in their State. We had a good laugh, and I realized one man's region beyond is another man's state next door; that to them, Maine was a region beyond!

So come with me to an era long since passed, and join two young men (21 and 20) as they move far outside their 'comfort-zone' and into 'the uttermost part of the earth' (Acts 1:8) for the first time. I wrote this as a bio for the publishers:

Have you ever wondered what it would be like to travel to a far off and distant place to share with an unreached people group the Gospel of the Lord Jesus Christ? "The Region Beyond" is a journey with two young cousins to the remotest mission station in the world in 1972. Travel with Barry and Bob Blackstone from Northern Maine to the Gibson Desert of Western Australia, exactly half-way around the world from their native homeland; there to feel another culture and climate far beyond their imagination or expectation. Experience with them their first overseas flight across the width of the great Pacific; journey with them into the barren wilderness that is central Australia on a day and a half railroad ride; fly with them through the interior of Western

The Region Beyond

Australia were mile after mile is nothing but flat, open wasteland; work with them on a million and a quarter acre sheep and cattle station and witness up close and personal the struggles of such a hostile land; drive with them deeper into the desert to an isolated community of Aboriginal natives and a few missionaries, and share with them the ups and downs of living in a strange land for a summer. The spiritual adventure will include a kangaroo hunt, dust storms that blotted out the sun, teaching aboriginal children the Story of Jesus, building a laundry and shower building in the heat of a hundred degree Australian "winter", catching, by running after a caboose, a train heading east at a desert junction, watching a tribal fight with spears and knives, and experiencing the hospitality of fellow believers that will only be duplicated by a trip to India. Learn what it takes to be a missionary to "The Region Beyond", and discover your life's calling despite the desire to return. On the 40th anniversary of this marvelous trip, the author recalls the events that made this memorable summer of '72 possible, and the lasting effects of this journey into "The Region Beyond"!

1

The Land Down Under

Revelation 7:9: "After this I beheld, and, lo, a great multitude, which no man could number, of all nations, and kindreds, and people, and tongues, stood before the throne . . ."

I STILL REMEMBER THE first time I attended the Prayer Band for Australia on the campus of Bob Jones University in Greenville, SC. I had given my life to Christ for full-time Christian service halfway through my freshman year. I had struggled since November 3, 1968, the night I first heard the Lord call my name for His service. I still have the old Bible that contains the message God gave to me through the preaching of my childhood pastor, Relland Clark. I had preached my first sermon in 1965 and had been encouraged by Pastor Clark to serve the Lord. I did that at my home church in Perham, Maine, but I resisted the call to full-time service. I wanted to be a lay preacher like my Uncle Read, and besides, my Uncle Sam was calling (the Vietnam War was burning hot). My generation's war was at its peak, and my father had been a soldier in World War II, so I also would do my duty to homeland and county; or so I thought!

Fulfilling a final request of my mother, I promised to attend one year of Bible school before I enlisted into the United States Army. There would still be time for me to fight. My first semester at Bob Jones was an eye-opening experience as I realized there was another army that needed recruits. I can say without a hint of doubt that I did not volunteer for God's service but was drafted into His work. Through a message delivered by Jack Van Impe at a local Baptist church in Greenville, I returned to the campus with my heart on fire to serve God and God alone. Uncle Sam would have to find another soldier, for I would only go to a far-off country as a soldier in God's army (II Timothy 2:3–4). I recalled the words of W. S. Brown and the music of Charles Gabriel that I had sung all my life, but now each word was personal:

> "A call for loyal soldiers comes to one and all; soldiers for the conflict, will you heed the call? Will you answer quickly, with a ready cheer; will you be enlisted as a volunteer? Yes, Jesus calls for soldiers who are filled with power, soldier who will serve Him every day and hour; He will not forsake you, He is ever near, will you be enlisted as a volunteer? He calls you, for He loves you with a heart most kind, He whose heart was broken, broken for mankind; now just now He calls you, calls in accents clear, will you be enlisted as a volunteer? And when the war is over and the victory won, when the true and faithful gather one by one, He will crown with glory all who there appear, will you be enlisted as a volunteer? A volunteer for Jesus, a soldier true! Others have enlisted, why not you? Jesus is the Captain, we will never fear; will you be enlisted as a volunteer?"

Since that first draft, I have volunteered ever since, including for the battlefield of Australia!

For the next year, I was active in an extension ministry in Athens, Georgia. Every Sunday through the second semester of my freshman year, I traveled farther (about 100 miles) south to minister to people who were shut-in (nursing homes) and shut-up (jails). It was my first real taste of ministry, and I found I loved serving God. It was about that time I also started attending the Prayer Band. Each evening after supper, groups of students would meet in different rooms in the academic building on the campus of Bob Jones University to pray for different parts of the world. Because I had never before had an interest in such praying, I stopped at the first room. (The rooms down a long hallway were arranged in alphabetical order according to the country being prayed for, and the first country was Australia.) What began on that first night was a love for the unreached people of Australia, and to this day, despite the fact God never called me to minister among them again, I still pray for 'The Land Down Under.' My heart's desire is that they would turn to God, and I know that one of the 'nations, and kindreds, and people, and tongues" that will one day stand before the throne of the Almighty will be the people of Australia and that land's native people: the Aboriginals.

It was at that Australia Prayer Band that I first understood Christ's 'great commission' to go into "all the world" (Mark 16:15) with the Gospel of Christ. Little did I realize that first night that I would be called to make a trip into this region beyond?

2

God Gives Another Aaron

Exodus 4:14: "And the anger of the Lord was kindled against Moses, and he said, Is not Aaron the Levite thy brother? I know that he can speak well. And also, behold, he cometh forth to meet thee: and when he seeth thee, he will be glad in his heart."

EVENING AFTER EVENING, I attended meetings to pray for the people and missionaries of Australia. As the weeks turned into months, and the months added up to a year and more, the Lord began to place in my heart a love for this distant land and its strange people. At the same time I met Wally Jarworski, a young man in my society of Basilean and the head of the Prayer Band for Australia. Wally was getting ready for a short-term mission trip to the Queensland area of eastern Australia in the summer of 1971. The more I talked to him, the more the Lord suggested that I could also make such a trip. But I quickly put that thought out of my heart and mind, as if I hadn't heard His call!

The school year of 1970–71 passed, as did the summer of '71. When I returned to Bob Jones University for my junior year, Wally was one of the first people I ran into. All he could talk about was his summer missionary trip to Australia. Once again the Lord began to move in my heart. I fought it for a couple of months, and like Moses, had every excuse in the book of 'why-not-me.' My last excuse was that I couldn't go it alone, and wouldn't you know it—an Aaron was being prepared.

My best friend and closes cousin was Bob Blackstone. We had the same great-grandfather and were both raised in northern Maine by farming parents. Plus, our high school sweethearts were next-door neighbors! We had attended the same high school and played ball on the same teams through three years of high school. I was a year older, but by the fall of 1971, we were both attending Bob Jones University. To help with our college expenses, we both worked for the maintenance department at BJU: me in the paint shop, and Bob as a mechanic. Each Saturday we would walk together to our appointed place of work and talk. On one such walk, our talk turned to Australia!

Little did I know that while the Lord was working on my heart about Australia, He was also working on my cousin's heart? Bob had joined the same Society I had and attended the Australian Prayer Band with me. He had met Wally, and the spark that had been lit in me had also been ignited in Bob. As we walked to work that pleasant Saturday morning, we both were without excuse. It was then and there we agreed that by the summer of '72, we both would work for the Lord in Australia, the first summer of our lives we would not work on our fathers' farms in northern Maine. It was a vow to each other and to our Father above: from then on, He would be our Boss. We had heard His call!

3

Where in Australia to Go?

Romans 15:20: "Yea, so have I strived to preach the gospel, not where Christ was named, lest I should build upon another man's foundation."

WITH THE DIE CAST, Bob and I started planning for our great spiritual adventure. But where in the great land of Australia should we go?

We approached the school to see if they were going to put an Australia team together for the summer of '72. They were, if they could get enough people to go. (At that time, there were two other girls interested in retracing Wally's steps.) We also talked to Wally about returning to the area he had gone to in the summer of '71, but the more Bob and I found out about Australia, the more our hearts were drawn to out-of-the-way places in Western Australia—a place no team had visited before. We were country folks from the back lanes of northern Maine, not city folks. We felt more called to the outback than the back alleys of Australia's big cities, but where to go and with whom to work? Some of our answers arrived with a native Australian who came to BJU to promote the need for missionaries to his country. His name was Pastor Dallas Clarnette of the Kew People's Church in Victoria, Australia.

Bob and I had stopped at his display during the mission conference and began to talk. We were both taken by his fiery desire for reaching his and other native peoples of Australia, the Aborigines. As we talked, we told him of our plans for the summer of '72. We parted that day with this agreement: if we did make it to Australia, we would first look him up so he could introduce us to a mission board that worked with Aboriginal groups. Our course was set to spend the summer with the people of the great Gibson Desert of Western Australia. We, like Paul, would preach the Gospel to an untouched people in a region beyond.

It was this early introduction to Paul's precept printed above that misled me in a belief that would take me nearly eight years to get out of my spiritual system. Despite having accepted Christ as my personal Savior at age seven, I was ignorant of this teaching of Paul:

> "I have planted, Apollo's watered; but God gave the increase" (I Corinthians 3:6).

I wanted to be a 'planter,' to start a pioneer work. (Which I did the summer after I returned from Australia in Pembroke, NH, under BJU's Church Planting Mission.) But what I didn't know then was that I was a 'waterer,' not a planter, and I have been ever since 1979 when I came to a fuller understanding of my spiritual gifts and callings. The good news in all this is:

> "So then neither is he that planteth anything, neither he that watereth; but God that giveth the increase. Now he that planteth and he that watereth are one . . ."
> (I Cor. 3:7–8).

It was through experiences like Australia and my first and only church plant in New Hampshire that the Good Lord was allowing me to grow into my spiritual gifts. It is so clear now, but when one is taking baby steps in the ministry only the steps are important, much more so than the destination even if that destination is "the region beyond"!

4

But My God Shall Supply

Philippians 4:19: "But my God shall supply all your need according to his riches in glory by Christ Jesus."

I AGREE WITH W. Phillip Keller when he wrote in his book, *Walking With God*, that:

> "Two thrilling themes traverse the timeless truth of God's Word. They run like a parallel set of footprints across the sacred pages of Scripture. They are imprints left upon the sands of human history by God and man. The first theme clearly shows us the generous, gracious, loving steps God himself has taken . . . the second theme . . . all through the ages; God has extended a warm welcome to wayfaring men to join Him . . . He has extended His hand to any who would turn towards Him . . . He calls us to joyous days and His own highways. There is new terrain waiting to be explored, new horizons to reach, new heights to climb in His Company."

I learned this and so much more on my first adventure with God to a far off and distant land to *The Region Beyond*!

After my cousin Bob and I determined to spend a summer in Western Australia ministering among the Aborigines, the real test of our trust began. How will God do it? Bob was in his

But My God Shall Supply

second year of college, and I was in my third, neither of us with any money. If we were to make our pilgrimage to Australia, we would need help. For the first time in our lives, we put our financial trust in the all-powerful hands of God. Up to this point in my life, I had never really had to trust my heavenly Father with money matters. My family was not rich, but we had the means to provide, through our farm, the necessities of life. Anything extra I worked hard for, so when I had a need or want, it would be supplied. For 14 years, this had been my relationship with God (since my conversion in 1958). Oh, I prayed for 'my daily bread,' but I saw the farm and my folks as the means to every end.

Bob and I determined, however, that if we were going to Australia for God, we would claim the great promise delivered to the Church through the pen of Paul, quoted above. It was my first experience claiming God's promises, but I knew if I were to walk with God through the unknown in an Australian desert, I would need to learn to trust his "exceeding great and precious promises" (II Peter 1:4). And through the fall of 1971 and the winter of 1972, the funds for going to Australia only grew as we shared with family and friends our desire to winter (when it is summer in the northern hemisphere, it is winter in the southern hemisphere) in Australia in the summer of 1972. Our theme song for that year of preparation was Paul Rader's wonderful, but simple chorus:

> "Only believe, only believe; all things are possible, only believe. Only believe, only believe; all things are possible, only believe."

What I learned about the provision of God that year has sustained me through nearly 40 years of pastoring poor, yet rich (Revelation 2:9), churches. I have never lived with excess, but I can confidently say that not once has my God failed to supply my every need, or the needs of my family and the church family under my charge, ever since the day I started to walk hand-in-hand with the Almighty God! Before you can learn to trust God in a region beyond, you must first learn to trust Him at home!

5

Thirty-One Dollars and Fifty Cents

Zechariah 4:10: "For who hath despised the day of small things?"

EVENTUALLY, THE SHORT-TERM MISSION team from Bob Jones University to Australia in the summer of 1972 numbered three: Virginia Vough from Markleton, PA, who was heading to Queensland; my cousin, Bob Blackstone from Woodland, ME; and me, hailing from the tiny hamlet of Perham, ME. Bob and I were heading to the great outback of Western Australia, final destination unknown! All we knew it would be a region beyond the cities and towns of Western Australia; an out-of-the-way place like were we came from, like Aroostook County!

As the plans for this great adventure began to come together, the biggest obstacle was the money needed to make the trip. The details for the flights to Australia were worked out through a travel agency in Greenville, SC. I was shocked when the combined total, just for the tickets to Australia and back, came in at $4,640 for the three of us. Today that might not sound like a lot of money, but in 1972 it was a fortune. Two years of college at Bob Jones only cost $5,000! I could tell you many stories of how the Lord provided that sum and traveling money besides, but I choose to relate only one story concerning God's ample supply.

Thirty-One Dollars and Fifty Cents

Besides money, certain documents also had to be supplied, including passports and visas. With our departure date advancing quickly, the money for the tickets was coming in nicely, but the paperwork was lagging behind. The deadline for the paperwork for our passports was May 1. On April 30th, Bob and I were still $30 short of the money needed for our passports. It might not seem like a lot of money to you but it was more than we had then. We decided not to tell anyone about this need, for we were confident that a parent or friend would supply, but we wanted to see God work. If we couldn't trust our Lord, our Lord alone in the United States, how could we trust Him in a place where we only knew him?

May 1, 1972 fell on a Monday. The day before, Bob and I went on our weekly extension ministry to Athens, GA, where we conducted services in four nursing homes and three jails. It was always a before-sunrise, until-late-in-the-afternoon Sunday. I was confident that somewhere in our travels that day the Lord would work, but when we returned to campus we were still without the $30 we needed. We quickly went to our post office boxes, thinking that perhaps the Lord would send it in the mail—but He didn't. Returning to our dorm, Bob and I were met by a friend who knew of our summer plans. Without a thought, he asked if we would be interested in speaking about our trip to a small church where he was ministering. We traveled to that church and spoke, and before we left, an elderly deacon shook my hand and with his other hand, put some money in my pocket. On our way back, I counted the gift, which totaled $31.50. I will never forget what Bob said when I told him the figure:

"Passport money and enough for gas!"

Over the years I have found God will not only supply a need, but seems to give a bit more. It is the lesson of the feeding of the five thousand (Matthew 14:13–21) and the four thousand (Mark 8:1–9); not only enough so all were full, but left-overs as well. We serve the God of the left-overs, even if it is only a buck and a half!

6

The Day of Departure

Proverbs 3:5–6: "Trust in the Lord with all thine heart; and lean not unto thine own understanding. In all thy ways acknowledge Him, and He shall direct thy paths."

THE TICKETS HAD BEEN purchased, the travel plans made, and the date of departure set: June 5, 1972. Bob and I were to fly out of Presque Isle, Maine, to meet Virginia Vough in California before flying on to Australia together. But as in any spiritual adventure, "Satan hindered us" (Thessalonians 2:18)!

Ever since my cousin Bob and I had decided to follow Jesus to the outback of Australia, we had faced obstacles. Sometimes it had to do with money, and other times it had to do with members of our families. I will be honest and say that not everyone thought a trip to the unknowns of a foreign country (The Region Beyond) halfway around the world was a good idea. Remember, Bob and I had only one contact in the entire country of Australia, and we had only met him once! There were a whole lot of unanswered questions for a couple of country boys who had never been on a plane before, or traveled outside America before? We didn't even know where we would rest our heads after we left the airplane in Melbourne! Many thought we were on a fool's errand, a crazy adventure, a silly quest, but deep in our souls that "still,

The Day of Departure

small voice" (I Kings 19:19:12) kept saying, "Go to Australia and I will guide you!"

My mother had often given me the verses I have printed at the beginning of this entry, but I never had a chance to really test them out until the spring of 1972. When I was asked when, where, who, and how, all I could answer was why! So as the day of departure grew closer, Bob and I returned from Bob Jones University to make our final plans for Australia from our homes in Maine. We packed our bags, put a few bucks in our pockets (less than $200 each—crazy, I know, for a 10-week stay in a strange land, not knowing where we would sleep or what we would eat), and packed our passports, but one important item was missing: our visas to get into the land of down-under.

Without our visas from the Australian Embassy in Washington, D.C., we couldn't get into the country. We had made our application in plenty of time, but as we left Greenville, SC, a week before our departure date, still no visas had come. Through the first four days of June we checked the mail and called the embassy, but still no visas. The hour of departure came, and still no visas. We had to call the travel agent to change our tickets, and some said it was a sign that we shouldn't go; yet in the noon mail on the day we were to leave, they came. We felt it was just another test from God concerning our resolve about going! Because we were to leave early on the morning of the 5th, we still had to change our flights. And in 1972, there were only two flights a week to Australia from the west coast of the United States, so it took some doing, but instead of giving up and giving in, we just kept trusting!

Today as I write these memories of forty years ago, I am reminded of that great chorus that goes:

> "I just keep trusting my Lord as I walk along; I just keep trusting my Lord and He gives a song. Though the storm clouds darken the sky over the heavenly trail; I just keep trusting my Lord, He will never fail! He's a faithful friend, such a faithful friend. I can count on Him to the very

The Region Beyond

end. Though the storm clouds darken the sky over the heavenly trail; I just keep trusting my Lord, He will never fail!"

I can see now that my trip to Australia was over a 'heavenly trail' with God leading all the way!

7

Walking by Faith and Not by Sight

II Corinthians 5:7: "For we walk by faith, not by sight."

JUNE 5, 1972 IS the first day I can honestly say that I walked by faith and not by sight. I had been a born-again believer since 1958, but I had never walked totally by faith until I came face-to-face with a spiritual trial that could only be handled with faith.

When the visas for our trip to Australia didn't come in the mail on June 4, I was cut to my heart with doubt and questions. Bob was the strong one who kept saying that everything would work out, but I couldn't believe the Good Lord had brought us this far only to delay our departure. I know now that God is as much in the "delays" as He is in the" starts", but on that day I questioned. I see now that my heavenly Father was teaching me about walking with Him (I John 2:6). I had set the date and made the schedule, but He wanted me to understand that this trip was on His time and according to His schedule. It was an important lesson to learn at the beginning of this trip, not in the middle or the end. (You will understand this concept better if you read on in this book!)

As Phillip Keller puts it, walking with God is "the powerful, pulsing principle that permeates all of life!" If I was to understand the change of plans, I had to realize that walking in partnership with another means harmony of timetables:

The Region Beyond

> "Can two walk together, except they be agreed?"
> (Amos 3:3).

The answer is no, and I had to learn that. I had to realize that walking in companionship with another means the sharing of time. I was now on God's stopwatch, and He had the will and the power to start and stop me without a moment's notice. I was now sharing a path and purpose, and my will and ways were no longer important to the plan. I had to realize that walking in stewardship with another means exercising trust. As Joshua had to learn to trust the Almighty as he ventured into new territory (Joshua 1:7–9), as Abram had to learn to trust the Almighty as he traveled to Canaan (Genesis 12:1–3), and as Moses had to learn to trust the Almighty as he returned to Egypt (Exodus 4:19–20), so too I needed to trust the Lord as I moved into the unexplored areas of His mission field in Australia; His Region Beyond, not mine!

As Bob and I waited two more days to depart, I was taught in that time that walking with God means separation. Keller says:

> "God calls us to walk with Him . . . away from the cozy comfort of our conventional little circle of companions."

We call that our 'comfort zone' today, and it is no easy matter to leave family and friends, yet to walk with God sometimes we must (Luke 14:25)! It was also during that waiting period that I learned the best lesson of all: that walking with God means clarity of mind, glorious peace, and an understanding, that without a shadow of doubt, that God can and does walk and talk to you. As Bob and I boarded a small plane in the Presque Isle Airport, I felt the first touch of the Hand of God on my life as we headed west for a very special rendezvous in the unknown regions of the Gibson Desert. I can honestly say that since that day, I have walked hand-in-hand with God! Oh, I have paused every once and a while to wonder, but quick to my mind were my days in Australia were I walked with God. My conclusion: if I can walk with God in a region beyond, I can walk with God and live by faith and not by sight at home!

8

There is a Friend

Proverbs 18:24a: "A man that hath friends must show himself friendly: and there is a friend that sticketh closer than a brother."

Despite the 48-hour delay, on June 7, 1972, my cousin Bob and I took off from northern Maine for our short-term mission trip to Australia. As we winged our way south to Boston on the first leg of our trip, I thanked the Good Lord again and again for the young man sitting beside me.

By my very nature I am a loner. I have always liked being alone in familiar territory, but I hate being alone in an unfamiliar land. I get lost very easily (the only time I have ever gotten lost while hunting I was alone and I still remember the horror I felt), and I hate being lost! I would never have made the trip by myself. I respect those who can, but God knew and knows that I have always needed a companion at certain times in my life

In my youth, Bob was the brother I never had. I was almost 13 before my brother, Jay, came along and nearly 14 before my other brother, Michael, made his appearance in our family. Needless to say, they have been more like my sons than my brothers for most of my life. That is why I am so thankful that the great God, in all His divine wisdom, gave me a substitute in Bob. Not just a brother, but a friend.

Bob was almost a brother; he was a cousin. We share the same great-grandparents on our father's side; that also makes him a Blackstone. Our fathers' farms touched each other, and though our homes were in different towns, we still grew up together. Being only a year younger, Bob was old enough to be my brother. I was raised on a homestead where I was surrounded by cousins, yet Bob was different. From the beginning he was a kindred spirit. We were a matched set, like two peas in a pod. I was blond and he was dark, but like Jonathan and David (I Samuel 18:1–4), we fell in love.

By the time we went to high school, we were inseparable. We did everything together from working to playing to courting to fishing and hunting. When it came time to go to college we chose the same university in South Carolina. College was just a repeat of high school for us. We were part of the same society, the same prayer group, and the same work department. We teamed up in basketball, horseshoes (of which we were university champions two years running), and soccer, not to mention numerous other activities.

And now we were traveling halfway around the world together to give a summer of our lives to the Aboriginal people of Western Australia. Who else would I have gone with? Bob was my right arm, or was I his? I was his courage, or was he mine? Bob was my first friend, and I have had few if any since. As I looked at him in that small airplane, I knew only a friend would leave homeland and homestead and 'honey' (Bonnie) to go who knows where and live with who knows whom. I had aspirations for ministry, not Bob, he only wanted to be a potato farmer, and still does, yet a friend does what a brother won't!

It was for these reasons and more I have never had a problem understanding the concept that Jesus taught His disciples when He said:

> "Henceforth I call you not servants; for a servant knoweth not what his lord doeth, but I have called you friends; for all things that I have heard of my father I have made known unto you." (John 15:15)

9

The Marathon Across America

I Peter 4:12: "Beloved, think it not strange concerning the fiery trial which is to try you, as though some strange thing happened unto you."

NEEDLESS TO SAY, BOB's and my first airplane trip across the U.S. was a marathon (a 3,500-mile marathon!). Having never flown before, we made every mistake in the book, yet our heavenly Father helped us overcome every obstacle and mistake, even teaching us a few spiritual lessons along the way, so that we arrived in California in time for our flight to Australia!

Our flight from Presque Isle to Boston was uneventful, but the minute we boarded the shuttle from Boston to New York, our trials began. Handing our tickets to the agent, we never noticed that instead of only taking our ticket from Boston to New York, she also took our ticket from New York to Atlanta. Of course, we didn't notice it until we got to New York and started to board our plane for Georgia. We had no tickets! Today, I would know what to do, but at the time, a panic came over me. A ticket agent in New York quickly solved the problem, but to this day I remember my heart jumping into my throat as I experienced, for the first time, the feeling of being stranded in an unfamiliar place. The feeling only lasted a few seconds, but I knew I didn't like it. We also learned just *how careful one must be as one travel's along:*

> "*This is* a faithful saying, and these things I will that thou affirm constantly, that they which have believed in God might be *careful* to maintain good works. These things are good and profitable unto men." (Titus 3:8)

Soon, however, we were on the plane bound for Atlanta. I thought often as we winged our way south that it was strange we had to fly into the Deep South to get to L.A. It was then I learned that even when God is your travel agent, He doesn't always plot you a straight course. Certainly the way of salvation is straight and narrow (Matthew 7:14), but our service for Him can be twisting and turning and turbulent, to say the least. Our path took us through Atlanta, where there was another lesson for Bob and me to learn about long-distance travel; *send your things ahead:*

> "But lay up for yourselves treasures in heaven, where neither moth nor rust doth corrupt, and where thieves do not break through nor steal." (Matthew 6:20).

Nobody told us that when you travel, you can check your bags through to your final destination. So at each stop, we went to baggage claim to retrieve our luggage. There was no problem at Boston and New York, because we had plenty of time between flights. But by the time we reached Atlanta, our extra time was all gone. Of course, our flight to L.A. was on the opposite side of the airport from where our flight from New York had landed. By the time we retrieved our luggage, we only had a few minutes to cover what seemed like miles to our next gate. To us, the Atlanta airport was the size of our family's farm, and we had to run from the homestead to my home, nearly a mile and a half. We made it just in time, but I learned in Atlanta to *travel light*, whether on earth or on my heavenly trip:

> "Wherefore seeing we also are compassed about with so great a cloud of witnesses, let us *lay aside every weight*, and the sin which doth so easily beset *us*, and

let us run with patience the race that is set before us" (Hebrews 12:1)!

During out flight from Atlanta to LAX we had our first, but not our last, encounter with air turbulence, a scary experience. Yet our heavenly Father compensated for the unpleasantness with a spectacular view of the Rocky Mountains! *Godly trials have silver linings,* we have to just look for them:

"For his anger *endureth but* a moment; in his favour *is* life: weeping may endure for a night, but joy *cometh* in the morning" (Psalms 30:5).

10

A Threefold Cord is Not Quickly Broken

Ecclesiastes 4:12: "And if one prevail against him, two shall withstand him; and a threefold cord is not quickly broken."

BOB AND I HAD left our home in northern Maine at 7:00 the morning of Wednesday, June 7, 1972. Our travels had taken us to Boston, New York, Atlanta, and by 7:00 in the evening, Los Angeles. We had seen hundreds, if not thousands, of people, yet Virginia Vough was the first familiar face we saw all day!

Virginia Vough was a 20-year-old junior at Bob Jones University from Markleton, PA. She had traveled alone from her home in Pennsylvania to meet us at LAX for our evening flight to Hawaii, and then on to Sydney, Australia. I have joked over the years that Virginia was the only girl I ever flew halfway around the world with (that is until I flew to India with my daughter Marnie in 2007). Remember, I needed a companion, a comrade, but Virginia, other than from L.A. to Sydney, was traveling alone. We would travel the same route back together, but for the bulk of her summer, she would be alone with her God in small towns up and down the eastern coast of Australia in a place called Queensland. I have respected her determination and trust ever since, but for a short period—a few hours in the summer of 1972—we were part of a threefold cord.

Walking with God is more than vision and vista; it is actually heading out, pressing on, going where you have never gone before. So when Bob, Virginia, and I boarded our flight to Hawaii, we were no longer armchair servants of the Almighty; we were ministering by proxy as so many do today; we were planting our feet on new land, fresh ground. We were tramping on terrain never before touched by our feet. It was on that flight to Honolulu that I learned the real meaning of:

> "How beautiful are the feet of them that preach the gospel of peace, and bring glad tidings of good things! But they have not all obeyed the gospel" (Romans 10:15–16).

It would have been easy for Virginia to stay home. Her original partner had backed out. She would have to go it alone. Most would have accepted that excuse, but Virginia knew the importance of going. Even if she had only two feet, she would use them to share the Gospel.

For 2,500 more miles, we chased the sun on that very long day in June. We talked and laughed about the mishaps so far, yet through it all a strong cord of friendship and fellowship was forming. When you share certain experiences with others, a bond develops; and when those experiences have to do with the things of God, it becomes an eternal cord. Virginia Vough and I never have and never will experience anything together again until heaven, but on that Pacific flight, I came to understand why God's servants are such special people. If you ever get to read this, Virginia (we lost contact after college, and it is my hope that this book might somehow allow us to reconnect), I want to thank you for the help you gave me that first day into The Region Beyond!

11

A Short Stay in Eden

Ezekiel 28:13: "Thou hast been in Eden the garden of God..."

I HAVE BEEN TO Hawaii twice in my life. Perhaps the closest place to the garden of God I ever found in my life (until I traveled to the State of Kerala in India) was those islands in the Pacific. It was the summer of 1972, and my cousin Bob and I were off to a missionary adventure to the land down under. We were to spend two and a half months working with an Aboriginal tribe in the Gibson Desert of Western Australia. To get to our destination, we literally had to fly halfway around the world.

From the northern hemisphere to the southern hemisphere, we went from summer to winter and back again. Starting from our hometown in northern Maine, we eventually arrived at the Warburton Range Mission Station. If you get out your world globe and put your finger on Presque Isle, Maine, and then your other finger on Warburton, Australia, you will discover that your two fingers are directly opposite each other. To get there, however, we had to go through paradise—the Garden of Eden called Hawaii.

It was my first experience with the vastness of the Pacific Ocean. Being landlocked in Maine, I hadn't seen much of any ocean up to that time in my life. From the west coast of the U.S.,

A Short Stay in Eden

we flew to Honolulu. We were there only to change planes for the overnight flight to Sydney. Because we had followed the sun all day, it was still light when we flew in from the sea to the Hawaiian Islands. They were beautiful against the backdrop of the Pacific Ocean. I could see from first glimpse why so many people love to spend their vacation time in Hawaii. I even had a friend (Kevin Buttram) in college who was a missionary there for a few years. We taunted him about it, but I will never forget his reply:

> "Even paradise needs missionaries!"

With barely an hour layover, about all we were able to enjoy about Hawaii was the flight in and out and a few spectacular views from the airport. Ten weeks later, we would fly back through Hawaii on our way home. Coming in from the South Pacific, the islands were like a chain of emeralds against the ocean. My heart was struck again with the loveliness and lush vegetation of these rocks in the midst of a huge sea. But as before, our stay was very short. By that time, we were anxious to get home, so we didn't even think of staying over to tour the islands a bit. We were soon on our plane bound for the States, and the last I saw of paradise was a quick glimpse before our jet reached the clouds.

I have not returned to Hawaii and doubt that I will. My brief encounter with paradise has often reminded me of our first parents, Adam and Eve. How often I wonder if, after Eden, they didn't ponder their quick trip through paradise. They were so hurried in their desire for something better, to be like God (Genesis 3:1–6), that they rushed through the best place they would ever experience. I sadly conclude so did I!

12

The One Ocean Concept

Nahum 3:8:"…that was situated among the rivers, that had the waters round about it, whose rampart was the sea, and her wall was from the sea?"

I FLEW IN A DC-10 with my cousin Bob and our friend Virginia across the broad Pacific Ocean on the night of June 7, 1972. But it wasn't until I read this by Phillip Keller (one of my favorite inspirational writers) many years later that I learned of the oneness of the ocean:

> "There are some aspects of the ocean that 20th Century technology has opened up to our understanding with tremendous interest. One of these great discoveries is that all the water of all the oceans is in fact one gigantic fluid. It is in constant motion and movement, circulating by means of colossal currents from pole to pole and clear around the earth. The ancient idea that each ocean or great inland sea, such as the Mediterranean, was more or less a self-contained body of water, restricted roughly within its own continental basin and boundaries, is no longer valid. We now know for a fact that these great oceans actually flow into one another in gigantic subsurface rivers that make the Mississippi, Nile, or Amazon seem like mere trickles in comparison."

The One Ocean Concept

This has helped me to understand why so often in Scripture 'the sea' is mentioned, not 'the seas.' Nahum in his comparison above is contrasting Nineveh with the Nile and Egypt, but in his analogy he speaks of rivers and waters, not seas. It is THE SEA! The Psalmist says, "He gathereth the waters of the sea together as a heap . . ." (Psalm 33:7). Note again, plural waters but singular sea. I have checked numerous verses and this concept is clearly seen in the Bible. Interestingly, scientific reality long taught in God's Word is just beginning to gain acceptance in the scientific community. The Bible was right all along:

> "For all flesh *is* as grass, and all the glory of man as the flower of grass. The grass withereth, and the flower thereof falleth away: But the word of the Lord endureth for ever . . . (I Peter 1:24–25)

Man has always been slow to accept the Bible at face value, but once again, technology and tests have proven the Creator right.

So, what for us could be the meaning of this scientific precept? Is there some spiritual concept we should learn? For me, could the one ocean be pointing us to the One God? Man has for so long believed in the plurality of gods. Like oceans, separate beings interacting but distinct. The Greeks and the Romans and Egyptians had panoply of gods, as did the people groups of Canaan, and modern man is trying again to join all the 'gods' of the different world religions into one happy family of gods. But we learn clearly in Scripture:

> "Hear, O Israel: the Lord our God is one Lord" (Deut. 6:4).

Even in the New Testament, through the pen of Paul, we hear:

> "One God and Father of all, who is above all, and through all, and in you all" (Ephesians 4:6).

With one ocean, there is no room for another; and with one God and one Lord (Ephesians 4:5), there is no room for others. All other talk of other oceans and other gods is nothing but a lie!

13

Pacific Revelation

I Corinthians 2:9-10: "But as it is written, Eye hath not seen, nor ear heart, neither have entered into the heart of man, the things which God hath prepared for them that love him. But God hath revealed them unto us by his Spirit: for the Spirit searcheth all things, yea, the deep things of God."

ONE OF THE INTERESTING aspects of our trip from Hawaii to Australia was that we never remembered June 8, 1972. We left Honolulu airport late on June 7th, and when we arrived in Sydney the next morning, it was June 9th. So where had June 8th gone? It had gone by way of the International Date Line. As we flew from the northern hemisphere to the southern hemisphere, we crossed the imaginary line that turns yesterday into tomorrow. The direct, overnight flight of 5,600 miles opened my eyes to this wonderful concept about the Lord printed above.

There is a big difference between 'revelation' and 'divine revelation.' To me, simple revelation is God through His Spirit revealing some truth about Himself to mankind. 'Divine revelation,' on the other hand, is what the Word of God recorded for us in the Bible:

"Because that which may be known of God is manifest in them; for God hath shewed *it* unto them. For the invisible things of him from the creation of the world are clearly seen, being understood by the things that are made, *even* his eternal power and Godhead; so that they are without excuse. (Romans 1:20–21)

Now God might use His Word to reveal something to us about Himself, but His Spirit isn't limited by the Word. The Psalmist says that God's creation can also be used to reveal godly truth:

"The heavens declare the glory of God; and the firmament showeth his handiwork. Day unto day uttereth speech, and night unto night sheweth knowledge." (Psalms 19:1–2)

According to Moses, "God made the firmament, and divided the waters which were under the firmament" (Genesis 1:7), and as night overtook our flight, I saw in the vast expanse of space and sea this marvelous precept about my Lord in terms of a divine 'speech' and a heavenly 'knowledge'.

We were only a day into our spiritual adventure, and I had already realized that my Lord had prepared the way. I had already seen and heard of amazing things prepared for me. Oh, I knew that the Lord had prepared them for others as well, but it was as if the Good Lord had created the glory of the firmament 'for my eyes only.' As I looked out the cabin window of the DC-10 and watched the sun set for the first time over the Pacific Ocean, it was as if I was witnessing the first time the sun went down over that mighty sea. It was breathtaking, inspiring, and beyond description for this simple farmer's son. I believe now it was at that moment I fell in love with the 'oceans'. (Since that flight I have had the privilege of living beside the Atlantic Ocean for twenty-five years. I have also returned to the Pacific Ocean once more and the Indian Ocean three times!)It was at that moment I understood at least in part what Paul was saying to the Christians at Corinth printed above.

The Almighty Creator has made for us so many wondrous sights to be enjoyed. Why? Because "we love Him"! I know He loved us before we loved Him (I John 4:19), but that doesn't take away from the fact that He leads us to days in our lives, special days just to witness His mighty handiwork. Only a child of God can really understand the connection between nature and the Nazarene (Matthew 2:23)!

14

Australia Island

Isaiah 42:12: "Let them give glory unto the Lord, and declare his praise in the islands."

BOB WOKE ME ON the morning of June 9, 1972 with the exciting news that Australia was in sight. Our 10-hour flight was almost over as the captain of the DC-10 announced that we were winging our way over Sandy Cape, the first piece of Australia we sighted. Our flight path from there would take us over Hervey Bay and down the coast by Brisbane. The early morning sun was just bringing its full power to light as the mixture of sea and seacoast filled our small cabin window. What a sight as the hills of Eastern Australia merged with the surf of the South Pacific. For more than an hour we watched as the last part of our ocean flight brought us over Australia. We had arrived; we had made it!

Despite the fact that Australia is almost as large as the contiguous United States, and that it is considered its own continent (the only country in the world with a continent to itself), it is in reality an island of three million square miles. Virginia, Bob, and I made landfall at Sydney. It was also at Sydney that Bob and I separated from Virginia. Her travels would take her north to Queensland, where over the next 10 weeks she would work through seven different churches running child evangelism programs. (Over that time, Virginia was able to lead 25 young people to a saving knowledge of Christ! How many people have talked themselves out of a short-term mission's trip, and how many have not gotten saved because of it?) However, Bob and I boarded another plane for our flight down to Melbourne, another 500 miles south of Sydney. We landed at the airport at 10:00 that morning.

Located on Port Phillip Bay, Melbourne was a city of a million people when Bob and I walked out of the airport; two country boys in a strange land with only a name and an address between us and being lost in a far-off and distant land. Pastor Dallas Clarnette lived in North Croydon, but his church was in Kew. Before we left the airport, Bob and I exchanged our American currency for Australian money. At that time, the exchange rate was in their favor, so we didn't get back as much money as we gave. Our first experience with foreign currency was not pleasant! The Australian government was also changing from the old British monetary system with their shillings and pounds to an American-type system with dollars, quarters, and the like. While there, we were able to use both kinds of currency, and we brought back both sets of coins and bills as memorabilia of our trip.

Our first trip in Australia was a taxi ride from Melbourne Airport to the corner of Fitzwilliam Street and Lofts Avenue in Kew. There we found a simple red-brick building, The People's Church of Kew-Victoria. Dallas Clarnette wasn't there, but two young men from his Bible School were there to greet us. We were expected and welcomed like long-lost brothers. As I ponder that welcome, I am reminded of what John wrote to Gaius:

> "Beloved, thou doest faithfully whatsoever thou doest to brethren, and strangers (And we were certainly strangers to the people of Australia); which have borne witness of thy charity before the church: whom if thou bring forward on their journey (And we were certainly on a journey) after a godly sort (And they did), thou shalt do well: because that for His name sake they went forth, taking nothing of the Gentiles. We therefore ought to receive such (And they did), that we might be followhelpers to the truth." (III John 5–8)

15

The Evening and the Morning were the First Day

Genesis 1:5: "And God called the light Day, and the Darkness he called Night. And the evening and the morning were the first day."

WHEN BOB AND I arrived at the Kew People's Church, we were greeted by Dennis Hartman and David Boyd. They were two of four students attending Pastor Clarnette's church-run Bible School, Faith Bible College. It was a two-year course study with practical training in church work. Dennis and David showed us around the church as we waited for the pastor to come. We had our first Australian meal (curry and rice; I wasn't impressed but I ate it with a smile being aware of Jesus' instruction to His disciples:

> "And into whatsoever city ye enter, and they receive you, EAT SUCH THINGS as are set before you."(Luke 10:8)

with the boys. After the noon meal, Pastor Clarnette came and took us back to his home at 2194 Anthony Drive. It was Friday in Australia, and the weekend was already upon us. Pastor Clarnette had made arrangements for Bob and me to visit the headquarters of the United Aborigines Mission, but our appointment was for Monday morning, so what to do for the weekend?

Back to Clarnette's home, we met his wife and family and were told we would only be staying there for one night. A family in the church had volunteered to put us up for the time we were in Melbourne because the pastor's house was too small to house us. That first night in Australia we slept on the floor. It might sound hard, but with jet lag and the time change, both Bob and I slept like babies. The evening meal was wonderful, better than the curry and rice at lunchtime; I was thankful that most of what was placed in front of us was wonderful. One word sums up our first full day in Australia: hospitality.

Having never traveled before, I was not used to living in somebody else's house and having strangers fix my meals and provide for me. My trip to Australia taught me the best meaning of the doctrine of hospitality:

> "Distributing to the necessity of saints; given to hospitality! (Romans 12:13).

What Bob and I experienced in our first 24 hours in the land down under was a perfect example of Christian hospitality. Peter might have taught it:

> "Use hospitality one to another without grudging."
> (I Peter 4:9)

But the Clarnette's practiced it. They treated us like sons and served us like brothers. When I desired (I Timothy 3:1) the office of bishop, I learned that one of the characteristics needed was hospitality (I Timothy 3:2, Titus 1:8). I saw first-hand what it meant to be hospitable in Australia. I can honestly say that Bob and I were ALWAYS treated in a hospitable manner.

During our first evening and morning in Australia, Bob and I were given a taste of the treatment we would receive during our entire stay on the island continent. From Christian to Christian, church to church, and mission station to mission station, we were treated as the King's servants by the King's people!

16

Greater Love Hath No Man than This

John 15:13: "Greater love hath no man than this, that a man lay down his life for his friends."

IN OUR FIRST WEEK in Australia, we were taken for a tour of the great city of Melbourne. It reminded me of pictures I had seen of European cities: very old and a lot of granite. The traffic impressed me because it was the first time I had seen people driving on the wrong side of the road (I would witnesses this phenomenon again in England on a second honeymoon trip with my wife in 2003; a trip I have written about in a book entitled *Scotland Journey*). I also remember being impressed with the difference in how a hitchhiker got a ride. In America, a would-be rider would stick out his thumb, but in Australia, he or she stands beside the road and sticks out his finger. I have in my picture collection of Australia a photograph of my cousin Bob standing on a Melbourne sidewalk with his finger out as Dallas Clarnette drove up to take us downtown.

The highlight of our quick afternoon tour of Melbourne was a trip to the heart of the city to visit the Australia War Memorial. This huge granite monument was created on hallowed ground in the very center of this old city. It was built to honor the men and women who had served and died in the First World War.

The Region Beyond

It was in 'the war to end all wars' that the nation of Australia was numbered with the nations of the world for the first time. Some say they joined the brotherhood of nations during that great struggle thanks to the legendary courage of their soldiers. On the blood-drenched ridges above the Dardanelles, in 1915, the outnumbered Anzacs—as the Australian and New Zealand Army Corps were called—held their own against the Turks, and even attacked, dying by the thousands. It was only after the very few survivors were ordered back that the slaughter stopped.

It was for the supreme sacrifices of Gallipoli that this memorial was built. As we walked through the narrow galleries with their stands of weapons and uniforms, pictures of battle scenes, and portraits of famous commanders, we eventually arrived at the heart of this impressive structure. What we found surprised me, for in an empty granite room was a simple hole. At the bottom of that hole was a marble altar with these words:

'No Greater Love.'

It was then that Pastor Clarnette explained the idea behind the memorial. The center of the structure was built, and a small window placed, so that on the 11th month, on the 11th day, at the 11th hour, the sun would shine through the window and strike those words. Of course, the month, day, and hour are the exact time World War I ended. As I pondered the significance of this man-made building, I realized that it was for the very same reason that I was in Australia: to tell these people of a man who had also given His life for them in great love. The concept had been borrowed by the statement of Christ printed at the head of this chapter. The Apostle Paul would highlight and underline this precept in his classic book to the Romans by writing:

> "But God commandeth his love toward us, in that, while we were yet sinners, Christ died for us" (Romans 5:8).

Would we get a chance to share the real meaning of these three words to the people of Australia?

17

Starts and Stops

Psalms 37:23: "The steps of a good man are ordered by the Lord: and he delighteth in his way."

AFTER A WONDERFUL WEEKEND of visiting and worshipping with the saints at the Kew People's Church, Bob and I were excited to make our appointment with the representatives of the United Aborigines Mission. We felt our true calling to Australia was ready to begin. God had something else in mind!

On Monday morning, Bob and I took the train into the city with the pastor. While he was taking care of other business, Bob and I sat down with the head of the Australia-based mission and offered them our services for the summer. Pastor Clarnette had contacted them, and we had a letter from Bob Jones University telling them of our desire to labor among the native people of Australia. The board had received a letter from their representatives at Cosmo Newbery Station asking for some summer help. We didn't have the foggiest idea where Cosmo Newbery was, but we felt like Eliezer of Damascus (Genesis 15:2) looking for Rebekah:

"I being in the way, the Lord led me." (Genesis 24:27)

When asked when we could go, we said now, but the Lord had other plans for his two servants from Maine.

It was then we were informed there was a nation-wide train strike underway. They asked if we had the funds to fly, but we didn't. So we were going to have to stay in Melbourne until the strike was over, but how long would that be? Nobody knew. Once again we heard in our hearts our old society verse:

> "But they that wait upon the LORD shall renew *their* strength; they shall mount up with wings as eagles; they shall run, and not be weary; *and* they shall walk, and not faint." (Isaiah 40:31)

We were learning that God had a lot of stops and starts in His plan for us that summer. So, what were we to do while we waited for the end of the strike?

When Dallas returned to pick us up, he once again came to our rescue. "No problem," he said. We could stay with the Nowells, the couple who had taken us in over the weekend, until the trains rolled again, and we could work in the church's ministries. The school was having activities toward the end of the week, and for the first part of the week we could do some house-to-house visitation for him. So as we returned to the church from the mission, we realized that:

> ". . . my thoughts are not your thoughts, neither are your ways my ways, saith the Lord" (Isaiah 55:8).

Three days into our stay in Australia, the Lord was already ordering our steps in directions we never imagined possible!

I am thankful that in the early days of my service for the Lord, He taught me that He is in control of both our starts and our stops. I know now that our stay in Melbourne was part of God's divine plan, but as we arrived back at the Nowells' house, I must admit I wondered what the Lord was doing. Were we to go out west, or was there a ministry for us in the highways and byways of Melbourne and the surrounding towns of New South Wales?

18

Stranded in Melbourne

Isaiah 40:31: "But they that wait upon the Lord shall renew their strength; they shall mount up with wings as eagles; they shall run and not be weary; they shall walk and not faint."

THE NEWS FROM 262 Flinders Lane (the location of the United Aborigines Mission in Melbourne) was disappointing. We had been accepted as summer missionaries for ministries in Western Australia, but a train strike would delay our departure to a place called Cosmo Newbery. So now what? It was then Bob and I learned it is not 'now what?' but 'now wait!' It was then we also learned that *you can do a whole lot for the Lord while you are waiting upon the Lord.*

The verse printed above was Bob's and my society verse. We both belonged to Basilean, a boys' society at Bob Jones University. At every meeting we would quote Isaiah 40:31, so by the time Bob and I got stranded in Melbourne, we knew it by heart. But it was in Melbourne that it got into our hearts!

After the stress and strain of the last few months at college, the added pressure of planning a summer mission trip to Australia, and the jet lag of flying halfway around the world, the Good Lord knew we needed a bit of rest before we faced the harsh conditions of the Gibson Desert. So He allowed us 10 beautiful days in Melbourne ministering and being ministered to by some very godly people. We had hardly hit the ground when we were taken to a youth camp called Mayfield, where we became counselors to a group of Australian young adults. One of the first postcards I sent home was to my girlfriend and future wife, Coleen. This is what I wrote about Mayfield:

> "I thought I would get a few postcards off to the folks. Tell your folks I will try to get one off to them, but I have run out of them and we are out-of-touch with the city now. We are working at a camp by the sea. It is a youth camp. I have a cabin of five guys mostly my age. We have had a great time. Mr. Garlock (Frank Garlock, the founder of Majesty Music and a teacher at Bob Jones at the time, was in Melbourne, unbeknownst to us. You can imagine Bob's and my surprise when we walked into the chapel and saw a familiar face!) spoke last night. He is going to be here today and tonight and is showing 'Gateway to a Miracle' (Bob Jones' promotion film at the time). So it is a little BJU here this weekend. We went out touring yesterday; saw some great country; got some good pictures. I wanted you to know that I wrote our names in the sands of the Pacific. I did this on a beach at the southern-most point of Australia!"

The weekend Bob and I spent in a camp by the ocean allowed us to 'mount up' and soar for the rest of the summer. I learned again that the Lord is good even halfway around the world!

19

Melbourne Ministries

Ecclesiastes 9:10: "Whatsoever thy hand findeth to do, do it with thy might."

BESIDES WORKING AT MAYFIELD, Bob and I had a very active ministry while waiting for the railroad strike to end. We stayed in Melbourne from June 9–20. During that time, we lived with the Nowells, a wonderful family from the Kew People's Church. They gave us the run of their small house and even allowed us to go to the corner bakery to buy fresh bread every day, a definite highlight. The food was good, if not varied, and we had a clean, dry place to sleep. What more could two lads from America want than that: maybe, a taste of home?

 Besides door-to-door visitation, where I was literally thrown out of a house for the only time in my life, Bob and I shared our testimony and missionary plans with anyone and everyone who would listen. It was good training, but our hearts were still being drawn westward. To fill up the time, the Lord gave us a chance to experience two interesting trips north of Melbourne. The first took us to Numuraka, a 100-mile trip one-way, where we were the guests of Pastor Clarnette and Mr. McKisicke. There was a great debate raging in New South Wales over the coming union of the Methodist, Congregational, and Episcopal churches. These two men of God had been asked to share their opinion on the merger of these religious bodies. It was an eye-opening experience to the trends happening in Australia, and little did Bob and I realize we were watching the rapid advance of the ecumenical movement happening first-hand on a world stage!

Our second great trip into the heartland of New South Wales took us to Stratmurtan, about 140 miles north of Melbourne. We had been asked to share our testimonies and show our slides (Bob and I had taken pictures of Maine and the homestead to share with our Australian brethren. They were most impressed with our snow pictures!) to a new outreach of Faith Bible College. Dennis Hartman, one of the students at the college, had started a home church in the house of the Reynolds family. Mr. Reynolds was a dairy farmer, and because my family was also in the milk business, a connection was immediately made. We had a grand time getting to know this man, taking a walk around his farm, having fellowship with his family, and seeing his love for the Lord. However, the memorable highlight of the trip was what took place in a small village on our way to the Reynolds homestead.

Bob and I had been in Australia nearly a week and a half when we drove into Shepparton, and there before our eyes was a Kentucky Fried Chicken sign! We asked Dennis if we could stop for supper, our treat!!!!!! We had very little money, but the pounds, florin, and shillings we spent that evening were well worth it. I can't ever remember a meal tasting any better than that bucket of chicken! That meal, our hands worked mightily, for it was 'finger–lickin' good!'

20

Go West, Young Man, Go West

Isaiah 59:19: "So shall they fear the name of the Lord from the west..."

THE DAY OF DEPARTURE from Melbourne had finally come. To this day, I still don't recall what the railroad strike was all about (I do remember that a round-trip ticket of over 3,400 miles that took three days only cost Bob and me $100 each, including meals!), but I do remember clearly the day (June 20) that Dallas Clarnette and his family put my cousin and me on the train for Adelaide. It was like leaving home again!

The first leg of our trip to the deserts of Western Australia was an overnight train trip from Melbourne to Adelaide: 600 miles through some of the prettiest country I have ever seen. During the daylight hours of our trip, we rolled through beautiful farmland and pastures and woods. Despite the fact it was winter, there was no snow, and everything was very green and alive. We arrived at Adelaide train station, having sat up all night. We had a three-hour layover before boarding our next train for Kalgoorlie.

Little did we know that the mission had sent word ahead that we were coming, so to our surprise, when we disembarked from the train we heard:

"Mr. Blackstone, Mr. Blackstone!"

Waiting on the platform were Clive and Joyce Gronow, UAM missionaries in Adelaide. The Gronows took us to their home for a cup of tea and showed us their work among the Aborigines. They ran the Nindee Hostel, a home-away-from-home for Aborigine children sent away from their outback homes to high school in the city. We had a wonderful visit with this kind couple that treated us just like family.

Within a few hours, however, we were back on the train heading west. The next leg of our trip would take a day and a half and cover 1,100 miles. Up until Adelaide, the countryside had been lush and inviting, but after Adelaide—and especially after we passed Spencer Gulf—the sights became less and less inviting. Soon there were no more trees, no farms, and no hills, just rocks and dirt and a depressing, dull brown. I can honestly say the sights on the inside of the train were more appealing than anything I saw through the large picture windows on the train. Only after hours and hours of travel would we stop, and then only for a few minutes at places like Woomera, Tarcoola, Kingoonva, and Loongana. But each was the same: just a dirty, dusty, backwater village with a few metal buildings and what seemed like even fewer people. More often than not, nobody would get on, and we would push on westward.

Even if the sights were not pleasant, the sleeper train made our travel west very comfortable. We had three meals a day served in a fancy dining car. Our room was small, but the beds were soft, and I remember falling asleep quickly as if being rocked in my mother's arms. I also remember one of the highlights was the chance to buy a can of Coke: another taste of home in a barren land far, far away from home!

21

Straight and Narrow

Matthew 7:14: "Because strait is the gate, and narrow is the way, which leadeth unto life, and few there be that find it."

HAVING BEEN RAISED IN the hills and hollows of northern Maine, I had no way of knowing what Bob and I would experience when we crossed the Nullarbor Plain of Western Australia in our trek to the United Aborigines Mission station at Kalgoorlie.

For nearly 40 hours, we rattled through a wilderness of sand. For as far as the eye could see, there was no sign of life. The skyline was clear, and the land was void; to top it off, we traveled on the straightest (at the time) railroad track in the world. Three hundred of the 1,100 miles was dead-on straight: 300 dull, dusty, dirty miles. Over and over and over again, mile after mile, with no dips, drops, detours, or diversions. It was the most difficult part of our travels, and certainly the most boring part of our 10-week mission trip. And it was double the boredom when we had to retrace the same stretch of straight track on our way home.

When we were told we were on this 'straight and narrow' way, all I could think about was the verse printed above. It was then I realized the true meaning of what Jesus was saying in this famous verse. So, how does one stay on the 'straight and narrow' way that leads to life? The same way Bob and I got to Kalgoorlie:

we stayed on the right track. The rails kept us straight—those two rails (I believe we too have two straight and narrow rails to be our guides through life: the Word of God (Psalms 119:9–11) and the Spirit of God (John 14:26).) our train was rolling on. It was then I saw what I believe the Lord was trying to get across to me:

> "Enter ye into at the straight gate: for wide is the gate, and broad is the way, that leadeth to destruction, and many there be which go in there at" (Matthew 7:13).

This is my spiritual application to these verses:

I have never seen in my life, then or now, anything wider or broader than the Nullarbor Plain. I imagined trying to cross that waterless desert on my own. There were a million possible crossings, but each would end in death. There was only one way across, and in those days, it was but a single railroad track from Adelaide to Kalgoorlie. So it is with the dangerous journey to heaven. There are the ways of man that seem right, but they all end in death (Proverbs 14:12). Jesus is the track; Jesus is the railroad to heaven (John 14:6). Once you get on board, you have a place to rest (Matthew 11:28–30) and eat (I Peter 2:2–3). You are safe (John 10:28–29) and secure (Philippians 1:6) on the way to your destination. Despite the hostile world outside the Australian train, Bob and I traveled without fear, and so it can be on the trip to glory, for

> "The Lord is thy keeper: the Lord is thy shade upon thy right hand. The sun shall not smite thee by day, nor the moon by night. The Lord shall preserve thee from all evil" (Psalms 121:5–7).

I would be amiss if I didn't ask which train you're on; what track are you travelling; do you know your destination? I have given to you in this chapter the clear Biblical answer, but is it the answer you have given?

22

Anticipation

II Corinthians 6:9: "As unknown, and yet well known . . ."

OUR JOURNEY ACROSS THE southern desert of Western Australia, called the Nullarbor Plain, was coming to an end. We had traveled over 1,700 miles from Melbourne by train. Despite the 300 miles of straight track, there had been 1,400 miles of bends and corners and curves. It was during that nearly three-day trip on an Australian passenger train that I finally came to an understanding of 'the romance with anticipation'.

Anticipation is the true spirit of 'beyond the bend.' What we know and have seen often becomes dull and drab, like 300 miles of the same-old, same-old! Our daily path will lose its glamour and glitter as we repeat our wandering, yes even a 'wilderness wandering!' 'Beyond the bend,' with its uncertainty and unexpected sights, draws us onward, forward, and even westward to THE REGION BEYOND as we search for that "prize of the high calling of God in Christ Jesus" (Philippians 3:14). With each mile finished, Bob and I were coming closer to the end of the line, and for me, a rendezvous with my Maker!

God has made our lives much like a train trip across Australia. How terrible would our lives be if it was all just one straight track? Like the trip from Melbourne to Kalgoorlie, our lives are also a series of corners and curves; that is what makes life challenging. We never know what is coming up, but we know 'who holds tomorrow, and we know who holds our hand,' (Matthew 6:34) even in Australia.

Vance Havner has written:

> "Indeed, that is what faith is: confidence in God's future. We know so little of life, of truth, of God and destiny. Businesses crash, health fails, friends depart, cherished dreams collapse—yet somehow ... most carry on."

Yet all these things are often around the corner, beyond the next curve. I can't imagine having to see the entire Nullarbor Plain at once; how discouraging and depressing and disheartening that would be! Just a glimpse now and then was enough for me, and that is how God leads us along. So with our Bible in hand and the Spirit in our hearts and the Lord leading the way, we press on through farmland and forest land and desert land until we reach our destination. A bend in the track might bring pain, loss, or disappointment, but we know once we are around it, there lies a golden city, a watered plain, a marvelous adventure!

For the Christian, there remains the last curve, the final bend, the ultimate corner. The world calls it death, but the Bible calls it a "departure" (II Timothy 4:6). A life 'beyond the bend' even to a region beyond where there will be no more corners or curves, because we will be living with God in His desert-less place (John 14:2-3). Our journey will be over, our wandering done. Our walk along the winding tracks of life will end 'beyond the bend' at the throne of God by the feet of Jesus! Amen and Amen.

23

Kalgoorlie

Isaiah 14:4: "...the golden city ceased!"

To most Americans, Kalgoorlie is the place where the American Space Station finally crashed back to earth. But for me, Kalgoorlie will always be the place where Bob and I finally got off that train!

As in Adelaide, Bob and I were met by UAM missionaries, this time Wilf and Beth Douglas. The town of Kalgoorlie was in great excitement when we arrived late on the afternoon of June 22, 1972—not because of our arrival, but because it had rained. The desert town had gone through nearly four years of drought conditions, but the rains had finally returned, and when the waters fall the desert blooms. Our stay in Kalgoorlie was just overnight, but we had a chance to tour this famous Australian 'gold town' the next morning.

After another wonderful night of rest under the roof of some very dear Christian laborers, Bob and I were ready for the next leg of our journey, a hundred and fifty mile trek to the next mission station on the way to Warburton. It was during breakfast that we were asked by Wilf, one of UFM's top translators:

> "How would you boys like to get to Leonora: by train (8 hours) or by plane (1 hour)?"

Without a thought, as if we were speaking from one mind (Philippians 2:2), both Bob and I said at the same time:

"*Airplane!*"

Our 1,700-mile train trip had convinced us that the only way to travel in the outback of Australia was by plane. This would be our only chance to travel that way!

Sure enough, Mr. Douglas knew of a man heading for Leonora that morning, so we got in his car and headed for the small regional airport outside of town. On the way we passed the statue of the patron saint of Kalgoorlie, Paddy Hannan, and the man who found gold in Kalgoorlie in 1893. This Irish prospector was just the first of many miners from all over the world who came to Kalgoorlie for the yellow ore and stayed. When Bob and I walked the famous 'golden mile,' nearly $2 billion (yes, that is with a 'b') had been pulled out of the mines in Kalgoorlie by 1972, amounting to 65% of Australia's annual production at the time. What would that gold be worth today with gold nearing $2000 an ounce?

As Bob and I neared the dirt-strip airport, we both realized that the richest treasure of Kalgoorlie was not its gold, but the godly men and women of UFM. In a short overnight stay, we felt like we had known the Douglas' all our life. Their dedication to reaching the Aborigines with the Gospel was inspiring. I knew I wanted to be like them, and to work like them. Their heart for missions was in every word and conversation, and their desire to get the Word of God into the language (Wongi) of the people was foremost on their hearts and in their minds. To eventually see and hear the native people of Western Australia reading the Bible for themselves was the goal they had set, and little did Bob and I know that we would cross one of their crossroads with them while in the Gibson Desert.

It was then that Wilf Douglas introduced us to Rogar Wiley, another Christian who was willing to help two Americans get to their next destination! It seemed that at very junction our Lord had somebody waiting to help us along. Such is the case when you are led by the Spirit and moved by the heart of God.

24

A Wilderness, a Dry Land, and a Desert

Jeremiah 50:12: "... a wilderness, a dry land, and a desert ..."

THE NEXT LEG OF our journey to Cosmo Newbery took place on June 23, 1972. Rogar Wiley, a Christian pilot, was flying supplies into Leonora, where there was another UFM mission station. He was happy to carry along two strangers from America on the 150-mile flight due north of Kalgoorlie. But the desert flight nearly didn't take place.

As we made our way down the long runway, oil began to appear on our windshield. Just before taking off, Rogar had to pull back on the throttle and apply the brakes to abort take-off. After taxiing back to the hanger, Roger—both pilot and mechanic—quickly found the problem. Within the hour we were soaring over the western edge of the Great Victoria Desert. Our flight took us over miles and miles of sand dunes and isolation beyond description. We had a chance from low altitude to see what we would be living in for the next two months, and it wasn't Maine!

Within a short hour, we landed on a dusty strip of land outside the sleepy village of Leonora (population less than a hundred). There waiting to greet us were the Bennett's: a family of seven. They were the UFM missionaries in the area, leading a small Aboriginal church. Our stay in Leonora was short, as we were soon in Mr. Bennett's car heading for Mount Margaret Mission Station seventy miles away through more wilderness and desert. We would be spending the weekend with the Landams in another very dry land.

Arriving late that Thursday evening, we were once again welcomed like long-lost friends. Bennett stayed the night, and we had a wonderful evening telling the story of how two farmers' sons from Maine had ended up in the deserts of Western Australia. It was there we also had a chance to ask a few questions ourselves about the mission and the people we would be working with. UFM had been organized around 1900 to reach the 'original Australians' with the Gospel of Christ. At that time, nearly 130,000 Aborigines were scattered over nearly three million square miles of desert in that corner of Australia.

Among the Aborigines were many tongues and dialects, but the one being used in the territory of Western Australia was the Wongi dialect. At the time Bob and I visited the mission, they had 75 missionaries throughout Australia, with 22 of them in the area we would be visiting. It was then we learned a bit more about the Aborigine people.

The culture of the Western Australia Aborigines was quite ancient and unique. Very strong superstitious beliefs and practices were at the heart of their society, but despite the barriers placed in their path by their deep-rooted culture, many had converted over the years, and quite a few communities in the region had an Aboriginal church. Bob and I would have a chance at Mount Margaret Station to experience the routine at a rural mission church, and to do something neither of us had ever done before!

It is wonderful to know that no matter the place, isolated or inaccessible, that God's people had penetrated the darkness, broke down the barriers, and had established the Church in these regions beyond!

25

Something New

Isaiah 43:18–19: "Remember ye not the former things, neither consider the things of old. Behold, I will do a new thing; now it shall spring forth; shall ye not know it? I will even make a way in the wilderness, and rivers in the desert."

OUR WEEKEND AT MOUNT Margaret was an adventure in itself. After we awoke from a grand night's sleep, we had a chance to explore Mount Margaret Mission Station. Situated in a rocky Wadi, the station consisted of only a few buildings. There were four missionaries at Mount Margaret: three women and one man, along with a few Aborigines. The Australian government had built a reservation for the Aborigines on a hill overlooking the mission, but the empty structures were a testimony to the ignorance of the government to the ways of the Aboriginal people. The missionaries had tried to warn the authorities about the customs of the Aborigines but were written off as religious do-gooders.

It seems the Aborigines believe that when a person dies, his or her spirit remains around where he or she died. This was one reason the Aborigines were migratory. They moved from place to place to escape the spirits of the dead. After millions of dollars were spent to build nice homes for the Aborigines in the area around Mount Margaret, the tribe moved in, but they were only there a few days when someone died. Instead of abandoning the house, they left the entire complex and never came back. It was strange to see the empty complex on the hill, but it was our first lesson in the difficulties of reaching these people for Christ.

It was also at Mount Margaret that Bob and I saw the last phone we would see for the next two months. The phone lines ended at Mount Margaret. The power lines had ended at Kalgoorlie, and we were beginning to understand just where we were heading. Since we'd entered Australian airspace, Bob and I had traveled nearly 2,500 miles as the crow flies. We were getting farther and farther away from what could be called civilization, and we were not as yet at this mysterious place called Cosmo Newbery.

The highlight of our stay at Mount Margaret had to be the church service we attended on Sunday, June 26, 1972. I wrote this date down in my diary because of the event that took place at the end of the morning service. It was Communion Sunday for the missionaries and their Aboriginal converts, and when it came time to share the elements of the Lord's Body, Mr. Landam, to our surprise, asked Bob and me if we would serve the Communion. I had shared in the Communion ever since I had been born again in 1958, but to actually pass the bread and juice was a spiritual treat beyond description. To actually hand out the elements to our newfound brothers and sisters in Christ, both white and black, was an experience I remember fondly to this day: a 'new thing' even in a desert place!

At the time of this writing I am just five services short of my sixth hundredth communion. I have shared communion with shut-ins in their homes and in nursing homes. Most have taken place in the churches I have pastored, and though all have been meaningful, only two have been memorable: a grand communion with the collective churches of the Independent Gospel Baptist Churches of Kerala, India in 2006 (my largest, I shared the service with 22 pastors, and over three hundred members of their congregations), and a tiny service with the saints of Mount Margret Mission Church in a desert valley in Western Australia. Besides being my first, it was also the only one I have shared with my cousin Bob!

26

Cosmo Newbery

I Chronicles 4:10: "And Jabez called on the God of Israel, saying, Oh that thou wouldst bless me indeed, and enlarge my coast."

WE HAD HEARD THE name 'Cosmo Newbery' for the first time at the mission's headquarters in Melbourne three weeks earlier. All we knew about the place was that it was one of the remote mission stations of the United Aborigines Mission in Western Australia, and it was our planned destination. The missionaries there needed helpers, and we were to be those helpers for the rest of our stay in Australia. Despite being nearly a week on the road, or should I say rails, Bob and I were still 100 miles from Cosmo Newbery. But how would we get there? There were no buses out of Mount Margaret and no planes either. If we were to continue on, we would need a ride. It was then our Heavenly Travel Agent came through again. Monday morning, we found a Mr. Brown, the Native Welfare Officer in the region and a Christian, passing through Mount Margaret on his way to Cosmo Newbery, and sure, he would love to give two Maniacs a lift!

We left Mount Margaret on what we thought was the last leg of our 'incredible journey' on June 27. We first passed through Laverton, the last-known town on the road to Alice Springs by way of Ayers Rock. (Between Laverton and Alice Springs was nearly 1,000 miles. We would cover nearly half that distance before our trip through the deserts of Western Australia was finished.) Laverton was a mining and petroleum town of about 2,500 people, including an Aboriginal population of about 600. We simply passed through on our way to the sheep and cattle station called Cosmo Newbery.

We finally rolled into Cosmo Newbery at suppertime. We were met by Claude and Dora Cotterill, the UFM missionary and his wife. It was while eating 'cosmo steaks,' my kind of Australian food, off an open grill, that we learned where we were. Cosmo Newbery was a million and a quarter acre ranch (yes, that's 1,250,000 *acres!*). It was run by UFM as a way station for the training of Aborigines who wanted to go from a nomadic lifestyle to a more domesticated life. The ranch supported a thousand head of cattle and two thousand head of sheep. (In the United States we determine how many sheep or cattle we can raise on an acre of land, but in Western Australia it is how many acres does it take to raise one sheep or cow?) Besides the missionaries, eight Aboriginal families lived on the ranch. Cosmo Newbery was also the last gas station and country store between Laverton and Warburton Range Mission, 300 more miles northeast of the ranch. The complex consisted of eight buildings and 22 windmill stations scattered around the ranch to water the cattle and sheep. There were no fences, except around the station. The animals were allowed to roam free, but think about it:

Where could they go?

Once a year, they sheared the sheep for their wool and sold a few head of cattle to meet the cost of running the station. Compared to the 720-acre farm I had come from, the Lord had certainly 'enlarged my coast!'

27

Moving On

Acts 16:9: "And a vision appeared to Paul in the night; there stood a man of Macedonia, and praying him, saying, come over into Macedonia, and help us."

JUST WHEN WE THOUGHT our traveling days were over, the Lord dropped the surprise of the trip on us. Around the table on our first night at Cosmo Newbery, we learned that Newbery wouldn't be our final destination. A call for help (by two-way radio) had come in from Warburton Range Mission. There was a need for someone to teach a children's outreach group and help with the construction of a laundry and shower building. Because Bob was the mechanic, and there were also a few needs at Cosmo, it was decided I would catch the next transport into Warburton, and Bob would join me later. I did, however, have one experience in my short two-day stay at Cosmo Newbery that I will never forget.

We arrived near mid-week, and I had a chance to preach at the weekly prayer service. It was my first experience preaching with a translator (most of the Aboriginal children we met had been taught English in school, but their parents knew only a few words), Claude doing the translation, but the thing I remember most about the service at Cosmo Newbery were the dogs!

Dogs? Yes, Dogs!

As I watched the people arrive, I noticed their pet dogs didn't stay outside. As each family arrived for prayer, their dogs came into the small chapel behind the main building. Most Aborigine families I got to know had at least one dog, and the majority had two or three. They were their constant companions and went everywhere with them, including church. They were the best-behaved dogs I have ever seen, for each came in and laid down under the pew where their master sat; much like Amanda, the seeing-eye dog of Michael Griffin, one of my current parishioners. At first, it bothered me as I saw more dogs then people streaming into the chapel, but after my experience at Mount Margaret, I knew I had to adapt. If it didn't bother them, it shouldn't bother me. I can't tell you what I spoke on that evening, but I will never forget the next time I read Philippians 3:2:

"Beware of dogs."

I now have a different understanding of what Paul was saying to the churches of Philippi; I had been there!

Within 24 hours of my 'dog' sermon, I was riding a semi-tractor trailer into the outback of the outback. Kevin Ewing, a Christian truck driver who took supplies and drinking water into Warburton Range Mission, was traveling in on his weekly run. It would take us nearly a day to maneuver around 300 miles of sand dunes. When I say it took a day, I mean a 24-hour day. We would stay one night camped out under the southern sky, eating our supper and breakfast cooked over an open fire. Unlike the train ride through the desert, I really enjoyed my day out with Kevin. Besides showing me the Southern Cross, he taught me what it takes to serve the Lord anywhere He leads, including a distant land!

Perhaps, the biggest lesson I learned in Australia was the need of the believer to be adaptable to the differences in the Christian community. I didn't know the term then, but now we call it 'unity in diversity'! I have come to believe this is the meaning of the doctrine of forbearance (Romans 2:24 and 3:25).

Whether a service filled with dogs, or milk used in the communion service, it is not so much about the elements and the worshipers as it is about the heart and purpose of the participants. Kevin and I talked about the differences I had seen in my first three-weeks in Australia compared to American Christianity, and there were plenty, but nothing worthy of separation; oh, that we might realize that Christ built 'diversity into the unity' of His universal Church!

28

The Southern Cross

Galatians 6:14: "But God forbid that I should glory, save in the cross of our Lord Jesus Christ, by whom the world is crucified unto me, and I unto the world."

ACCORDING TO A LETTER I wrote my girlfriend, Coleen, now my wife, Kevin Ewing and I headed into the great Gibson Desert at 10:30pm on June 29, 1972. We drove until 1:30am before stopping by the side of the road (more like a sandy beach) to catch a few hours of sleep. Before we fell asleep, Kevin 'boiled the kettle' for a cup of tea. I remember it was a beautiful, star-filled night with no artificial lights to block the view. I remember it was a warm night, pleasant, the best winter's night I have ever spent out in the open. Even the sand was soft as I lay down beside Kevin's big truck for my first night's sleep under the stars in Western Australia.

As I gazed up into the dark canopy of space, my mind turned to the words of the Psalmist:

> "The heavens declare the glory of God; and the firmament showeth his handiwork. Day unto day uttereth speech, night unto night showeth knowledge" (Psalms 19:1–2).

It was then Kevin asked if I had yet noticed the famous 'Southern Cross.' I told him that I had been so busy looking around that I had not really looked up! Drawing my attention to a certain corner of the sky, Kevin then pointed out the Southern Cross. Sure enough, there in God's majestic heaven was a group of stars in the shape of a cross! Unknown to us in the northern hemisphere, Corona Australis is a southern constellation that pictures perfectly the symbol of our Faith. The greatest truth I saw in the Southern Cross is that there is no man still hanging on it. The cross of Christ is empty, and so is the Southern Cross!

My other impression of that southern constellation is expressed in the verse written by Paul that is printed above. Galatians 6:14 has been a favorite verse of mine and was already special when I went to Australia.

"God forbid that I should glory, save in the cross of our Lord Jesus Christ!"

The glories of the Southern Cross were everything I expected, and I must admit, more than I could have imagined. Added to the fact I got to witness its appeal laying on my back in a pile of sand in the early hours of an Australian morning only makes this comparison more inspiring to me. I hadn't come to Australia necessarily to see the Southern Cross but to proclaim another cross, one more glorious and eternal than a heavenly constellation. I am thankful I got to see the Southern Cross in its Australian beauty, but I am more grateful that in a small country church at the age of seven, I got to see the cross of Christ in its divine beauty.

I would see the Southern Cross for another few weeks, and then it was lost to me. The cross of Christ I still see, and I still glory in it!

29

Warburton Range Mission

Hebrews 11:38: "...they wandered in deserts..."

KEVIN AND I GOT up around 6:30am after a few hours of sleep and headed out again for the Warburton Range Mission. During the trip I was told we were heading to the remotest mission station, not just in Australia, but in the world at the time: 300 miles north, south, east, or west from any other settlement or human being. Even the 300 miles was 'straight as the crow flies,' and I noticed as we slowly made our way around and over and through the sand dunes that we were doing anything but going straight. I never actually recorded how many miles we drove, but it took us from 6:30am to 5:00pm to finally pull into Warburton, and that was in addition to the three hours we had driven the night before from Cosmo Newbery!

Warburton was not much to look at when I finally had a good view of my home-away-from-home for the next month (June 29-July 23, 1972). The mission buildings sat on a low plateau surrounded by a very, very dusty plain. A series of slightly higher hills could be seen in the distance (Warburton Range). The only reason UAM had planned a station in the area was the group of nearly 600 Aborigines that lived nearby. The Australian government had also built a school and store on the same rise of land. Some might have called it a small town, but it was more just a scattered set of buildings in a very deserted place. The natives were not even settled, wandering in and out as they searched for food and hunted for game. The government and the missionaries would provide food, but this particular tribe was still very primitive and independent.

I was greeted by Herbert Howell, station director, and immediately taken to a late afternoon prayer meeting where I met his wife, Lorraine, and son, Beven, who would celebrate his first birthday while Bob and I were there. I also met Ken and May Siggs, the child evangelism workers at the station. I would have many chances to work with them in the school through Bible clubs and children's meetings. It was at that prayer service I also got to know Amee Glass and Dorthy Hackett, Wycliffe translators working at the mission. They had actually pioneered the work by moving into Warburton to learn the dialect of this particular tribe, so the Bible could be translated into their language. These dear brothers and sisters in Christ would be my family over the next four weeks.

The strangest event of my first few hours at Warburton was the young Aborigines shouting my name when I arrived. To my surprise, the next mountain range (more like hills) beyond Warburton Range is Blackstone Range. That's right; I traveled half-way around the world to discover that the native Australians already knew my name because part of the territory they wandered in was called 'Blackstone!'

After nearly three weeks in the country, I had finally reached 'the region beyond' that I was looking for. It was isolated and a bit intimidating, but as with each stop along my journey I felt a deep, spiritual peace that I was in the right place, at the right time, for the right reason! I claimed again and understood again God's promise of peace:

> "Thou wilt keep him in perfect peace, whose mind is stayed on Thee: because he trusteth in Thee." (Isaiah 26:3)

I was trusting and I was at peace, even in this desert place called Warburton Range Mission.

30

Answer to Prayer

Psalms 91:15: "He shall call upon me, and I will answer him…"

ONE OF THE FIRST confirmations I received that I was supposed to be in Warburton was given to me the first afternoon of my arrival. Besides the kids shouting my name (the missionaries had told them that 'the Blackstones' were coming for a visit) was a statement in a prayer from one of the missionaries at that first prayer meeting.

It was part of the routine at Warburton to have a time of prayer during the late afternoon. As I gathered for the first time with this group of UAM missionaries, I felt very comfortable. I failed to write it down, but as I listened to the supplications and intercessions of my co-workers at Warburton, one of them started their prayer by thanking the Lord for the two young men He had sent in answer to their prayers! That surprised me because I thought when we left Melbourne that we were only going to Cosmo Newbery. After the prayer session was over and everyone had returned to their workplaces, I asked Mr. Howell (a young father not much older than I was) what was meant by the praise in the missionary's prayer. It was then I was informed that as a group, they had been praying for nearly a year for help in building a new laundry and shower room for the Aborigine women and their children. "A year?" I asked, to which Herbert replied, "Yes, a year!"

In that moment I realized just how 'worldwide' my God really is. If He could hear the prayers of a group of saints in another hemisphere, in a country halfway around the world, and answer that petition by speaking to two lads on the other side of the world. What a global God I was serving! That and the promise of "Again I say unto you, that if two of you (even two missionaries in the middle of the Gibson Desert) shall agree on earth (even in Western Australia) as touching anything (the need for two workers to build a laundry) that they shall ask, it shall be done (by moving two college kids from one side of the world to the other) for them of my Father which is in heaven" (Matthew 18:19).

I have never (as you can tell) forgotten that afternoon prayer meeting. It was a dramatic answer to prayer that has helped me believe that we can ask, and if need be, God will move heaven and earth to see that even the simplest of supplications are answered. It was in that same conversation with Herbert Howell that I learned that among the missionaries there was no carpenter, no electrician, no mechanic, and no real practically-skilled missionaries. I realized then that to be a missionary in a remote station on the backside of nowhere you needed more gifts and talents than just the ability to teach and preach the Word of God. I was beginning to learn that to be a servant of God in a primitive place, working with limited resources; you had to be both adaptable and able!

I was adaptable, but was I able? Once I saw the project before me, I couldn't wait the arrival of Bob, the able one!

31

Gibson Desert Aborigines

Jeremiah 25:24: "The mingled people that dwell in the desert..."

I WASN'T LONG AT Warburton when I learned my first lesson about the people I had come to reach: the Gibson Desert Aborigines.

The Aboriginal skin is dark, like an African-American, but their hair can be as blond as a young man's from Maine. They have broad noses and slender, small bodies. Aborigines are well-adapted to the harsh conditions of their desert home with strong teeth and heavy, calloused feet. The language of the Gibson Desert Aborigines is Pitjantjara, but a different dialect is found in nearly every tribal group. When Bob and I were there, 3,000 Aborigines were scattered over an area the size of New Mexico, which made the group at Warburton (600) one of the largest concentrations in the region; hence, the location of the mission.

Hunting and foraging were the primary occupations of these people, and they did this in one of the least verdant areas of the world. I couldn't understand where they could find any food, yet they did, and we were shown how they did.

"Can God furnish a table in the wilderness?"
(Psalms 78:19).

Gibson Desert Aborigines

I learned in the Gibson Desert of Western Australia that He can! While the men hunted the emu (like an ostrich)—or, as one man put it, 'a big feather duster on legs' (Bob and I did get to see one of these big birds in the wild, and it was running about 30 miles per hour!)—and kangaroo and other small game, the women and children would gather fruits like quandongs (a valuable source of nutrition) and wanguna seeds, which they beat into a flour to make bread.

Because of their wandering lifestyle and migratory manner, the Aborigines live with very simple things, all of which are portable. There were a few make-shift huts near Warburton, but no Aborigines lived in buildings. They came to use the store or school or laundry, but they either lived in the open or in small huts made of whatever materials they could find. Their tools were very simple as well, including spears (up to 14 feet long), clubs, wooden bowls (I still have one in my Australian paraphernalia), throwing and digging sticks, and of course, boomerangs. I soon learned that not all boomerangs are created equal, for there are two kinds: killing boomerangs that are thrown simply to knock down an animal or bird, and the traditional boomerang that would, if curved right, return to the thrower (I never mastered the art form!).

I also learned that the Aborigines were the last people group to use the spear thrower, which gave extra leverage in casting a spear. I witnessed some Aboriginal men throw their huge spears nearly 50 yards! Bob also witnessed these weapons being used not just in hunting, but also in warfare; another story for another time.

It was John in his revelation that made this observation:

> "After this I beheld, and, lo, a great multitude, which no man could number, of all nations, and kindreds, and people, and tongues, stood before the throne, and before the Lamb, clothed with white robes, and palms in their hands." (Revelation 7:9)

And numbered among that mighty multitude will be the Gibson Desert Aborigines of Western Australia.

32

Two are Better than One

Ecclesiastes 4:9: "Two are better than one; because they have a good reward for their labor."

HERE ARE A FEW lines I wrote to my girlfriend from that isolated Western Australia mission station:

> "Here it is the end of another week, and the start of a new month. July 1 is here and all is not well in Australia. Had a rough day; guess the devil won one. It was the hardest day on the whole trip. I guess I have settled down, and 'he' got to me. I wasn't really praying. I have time or make time to have my personal devotions, but still feel alone. You know what happens when I don't pray. I finished the door frame for the Howells' bedroom. They took off this afternoon to pick up Bob!"

Once the excitement of travel wore off, and the routine of being in a far-off-and-distant place hit me, I realized just how much I missed my cousin Bob. We had only been separated for a few days, but the support and strength that comes from sharing a load became apparent at Warburton:

> "For if they fall, the one will lift up his fellow: but woe to him that is alone when he falleth: for he hath not another to help him up." (Ecclesiastes 4:10)

Two are Better than One

During those few days of separation from my traveling companion and dear friend, I learned that I could never be a single missionary. I could not go it alone; I was in need of a friend, a comrade, or a wife! It was also then I noticed that to this point in our travels, we hadn't met a single, 'single' missionary. Even the 'single' missionary had a partner. Most were couples, but at Mount Margaret and Warburton, I met those who had come alone but soon partnered up with someone. In the great adventure of traveling into the Gibson Desert alone, I had come face-to-face with the Wisdom of Solomon:

> "How can one be warm alone?" (Ecclesiastes 4:11).

In my very next letter to my girlfriend I wrote:

> "Hope it is nice where you are. We are in the middle of a dust storm. The wind is blowing up the desert, and the camp is located on a plateau. Boy does the dust fly! Well, old Bob got in last night. We were saying that in the last few days we were alone for the first time. We both were lonely....... and it was good to be back together. It was good to have him come. He had a hard trip in!"

The Good Lord was teaching me and my cousin the importance of 'two.' It was not by chance the Lord sent His disciples out 'two by two' (Luke 10:1) and that the first missionaries went out 'two by two' (Acts 15:39–40). All of a sudden, within days of arriving at Warburton Range Mission, I was beginning to realize that maybe, just maybe, being a missionary was more complicated than I thought?

33

Feed My Lambs

John 21:15: "He saith unto him, Feed my lambs."

JULY 5, 1972 WAS a day to remember. In a small diary of dates, I recorded only 15 special days during my stay in Australia. This day I simply recorded, "Taught Bible story to 75 Aboriginal children!"

When Bob and I decided to spend the summer of '72 in Western Australia, we did not know what ministry opportunities we would have. We knew there would be a language barrier, so we accepted the fact that few chances of direct service would take place. When we finally got to Warburton, we discovered that most of the children knew English, having been taught it in the local public school. Just a few days after Bob arrived in Warburton, we were asked if we wanted to share a Bible story at a children's after-school meeting. It was after re-reading a letter I sent to my girlfriend Coleen that I recalled what I had shared with God's Australian 'lambs.'

According to my letter to Coleen, I spoke on II Kings 4:8-37. This scripture tells of the Shunemite woman and how Elisha raised her son back to life. I recall very little about that message or meeting except that we met in a large school room after school. Bob and I had been working on the new laundry and shower building during the morning and early afternoon.

Feed My Lambs

We stopped early in preparation for the Bible Club run by the Siggs. After that first hands-on encounter with the children of Warburton, I wrote to Coleen:

> "The children are fully clothed, but most of them don't wear shoes. The living conditions are really bad, but I have seen places almost that bad in the States. They are very poor; no work around here. They have a bad sanitation problem. They are very dirty people. The dogs seem to get more baths than the children!"

It was the children of the desert that touched my heart the most. To see their smiling faces in the midst of such poverty and poor conditions affected me to my soul. Their only hope was to find Christ. There was little or no hope for much of a life in the Gibson Desert. With the conditions and climate, the life expectancy was short; their only hope for a long life was eternal life. Despite the dusty wind and harsh weather, the children of Warburton played like all children. Their toys and games were homemade, but these precious 'lambs' were open to the Gospel. I remember the quietness and stillness in that first meeting, as if there was a hunger for the words I spoke. I can honestly say that I have been in many a meeting with kids, but no 'lambs' were any more receptive than these!

I have now spent a lifetime ministering to children; a ministry I never thought I had ability to perform. In just a few days I will start my 23rd year teaching 8–12 years olds in a youth ministry called AWANA. I have been youth pastor in nearly fifty summer youth camps to children of the same age and some a bit older. I have had the privilege to teach young people the Gospel from late teens to kids as young as three (a new ministry I started last year in AWANA to our Cubbies (3 and 4 year olds). The first service I ever conducted with God's 'lambs' was that day in Warburton; little did I realize the ministry ahead of me (at the writing of this chapter I have conducted over 1600 such meeting and by far I have lead more 'lambs' to Christ than sheep). I have taken seriously Jesus' admonition:

> "Suffer little children, and forbid them not, to come unto me: for of such is the kingdom of heaven." (Matthew 19:14)

34

Whatsoever Ye Do

Colossians 3:23: "And whatsoever ye do, do it heartily, as to the Lord, and not unto men."

WITHIN A SHORT TIME after our arrival at Warburton Range Mission Station, Bob and I were in a daily routine. Besides the afternoon prayer meeting and the after-school Bible clubs, we spent the bulk of our time fixing and building things. It was on that remote station that I learned the importance of Paul's precept printed above.

I recall one morning was spent putting new fuel injectors in the engine that produced electricity for the compound. The motor was only run for a few hours in the afternoon and for lights in the evening. It was an important piece of equipment at the station but hadn't been serviced for quite a while. When Herbert discovered that Bob was an auto mechanic and had worked on diesel engines, he was excited. They had received a new set of fuel injectors' months before, but nobody at the station knew how to put them in. Bob was the answer to another of their prayers!

Bob and I were also asked to play Australian football (a cross between soccer, rugby, and American football) with the Aborigine boys at the station. We had a chance to watch a game or two on television while we were in Melbourne, so we had some idea of how it was played. We finished work about 5pm and got back to the Howells' house to find four young boys waiting for us. Within a few minutes we were swamped with kids, and the game was on. I remember I was tired after 15 minutes! It's a very rough sport, and I landed on the ground more than once, but with each put-down, there were many dark, eager hands to help me up. When the game was over, I counted nearly 40 boys surrounding Bob and me. Sometimes you need to play a game of football to serve the Lord!

I also recall doing simple errands around the compound, and each time I would leave the house, a boy or two would follow me, just like puppy dogs. In one of my letters, I told Coleen that I had taken a typewriter to a missionary's house for Mrs. Howell, and when I got back to the Howell house, I had 15 boys in tow. The children at Warburton were very hungry for attention. It seems that Aboriginal adults are not very affectionate toward their children. Just sharing a few minutes with these children, even on a walk, brought them great joy; and I must admit it brought great joy to me as well.

One day Kevin Ewing came back, and Bob and I helped load his trailer with empty barrels. Everything, and I mean everything, had to be hauled into Warburton. One evening Mr. Siggs and I went out about three miles into the desert to find firewood and one of our tires fell off; we had broken the studs on the rough road. I remember having to walk back to Warburton to get help. I sang heartily all the way back!

Each of these events in Warburton might seem routine, they could have been done anywhere, but that is part of any mission work. I remembered well my upbringing:

> "Whatsoever thy hand findeth to do, do it with thy might ...." (Ecclesiastes 9:10)

35

One

Luke 15:10: "Likewise, I say unto you, there is joy in the presence of the angels of God over one sinner that repenteth."

AFTER POURING THE FOUNDATION for the Aborigines' new laundry and shower building, Bob and I began the metal and wood construction of the newest structure at Warburton. Morning and afternoon, until the very hot sun took its toll, was spent in putting this work project together. The rest of the time we spent building relationships with the people of the station. At each desert station where Aborigines lived was a Native Welfare Officer of the Australian Government. Mr. Brown had a young daughter, and it was to her that the Lord had sent Bob!

I had known the story of the lost sheep, the lost silver, and the lost son for most of my life. In out-of-the-way Warburton, Bob found the lost lamb of his trip to Australia. During one of the Bible clubs, the chief concept of this famous trilogy was demonstrated (see verse above). Bob had traveled halfway around the world to lead a little child to Christ. It seems strange that with a station full of missionaries, it was be a college sophomore from Maine whom God would use to lead this child to Himself.

It was events like this at Warburton that showed me that:

One

"My thoughts are not your thoughts, neither are your ways My ways, saith the Lord. For as the heavens are higher than the earth, so are My ways higher than your ways, and My thoughts than your thoughts. . . . So shall My word be that goeth forth out of My mouth: it shall not return unto me void, but shall accomplish that which I please, and it shall prosper in the thing whereto I send it" (Isaiah 55:8-9, 11).

God sent a young man around the world to share His Word with a young Australian girl, and the 'thing' that happened was a soul saved! We serve the God of the 'one.' Jesus went to Jericho (Luke 19:1-10) to seek and to save 'one' man, and he went to Samaria (John 4:1-10) to seek and to save 'one' woman. Bob went to Australia to lead 'one' little lady to a saving knowledge of Christ.

I have kept a similar story until this part of my tale because of how it parallels Bob's, but on June 15, 1972, while we were still stranded in Melbourne, I led a little Catholic boy to Christ while on house-to-house visitation for the Kew People's Church. While Virginia was able to lead many boys and girls to Christ on her stay in Queensland, Bob and I only saw these two 'lambs' saved. Yet in the light of Luke 15, it was worth the trip. To traverse ocean and continent for 'one' soul is what being a missionary is all about. Both Bob and I had been paid eternally for our service in Australia!

Forty years after these two events I wonder where these two individuals are now (they both would be in their forties)? There is a very good chance we will not see them again until heaven, but their story reminds me of the truth behind Ray Boltz's best known song, "THANKS":

"I dreamed I went to heaven and you were there with me. We walked upon the streets of gold beside the crystal sea. We heard the angels singing then someone called your name. You turned and saw this young man and he was smiling as he came. And he said, 'Friend, you may not know me now,' and then he said, 'You used to teach my

Sunday school when I was only eight. And every week you would say a prayer before the class would start and one day when you said that prayer I asked Jesus in my heart!' (You came to my home in Melbourne and before you left I asked Jesus into my heart.) Then another man stood before you and said, 'Remember the time. A missionary came to your church, and his pictures made you cry. You didn't have much money but you gave it anyway. Jesus took the gift you gave, and that's why I'm here today!' (You came to my home in Warburton and gave me the Gospel, and that is why I'm saved today.) One (a boy from Melbourne) by one (a girl from Warburton) they came far as your eyes could see. Each life somehow touched by your generosity. Little things that you had done sacrifices you made (a summer in Australia). They were unnoticed on earth, in heaven now proclaimed. And I know that up in heaven you're not supposed to cry, but I am almost sure there were tears in your eyes. As Jesus took your hand and you stood before the Lord, He said, 'My child look around you, for great is your reward!' Thank you for giving to the Lord. I am a life that was changed. Thank you for giving to the Lord. I am so glad you gave (of your summer in Australia)."

36

Blackstone

Psalms 78:52: "... and guided them in the wilderness ..."

AFTER BEING IN WARBURTON for a little over two weeks, Bob and I were given a day off. I remember clearly that it was a Saturday morning when Herbert asked if there was anything Bob and I would like to do while we were at Warburton, or any place we would like to go. Because we had seen and visited the Aborigine village outside of town, there was only one place and one thing we hadn't done or seen: a kangaroo hunt and a trip to Blackstone!

Herbert made arrangements with a very experienced Aboriginal Christian by the name of Rogar (I couldn't pronounce, let alone spell, his last name) to take Bob and me into Blackstone (a 134-mile trip, one way). It would take us all day to drive to and from the Blackstone Ranges, and maybe on the way we could kill a kangaroo for Sunday dinner. We were also hopeful that we might see a wild dingo, Australia's native dog. We had seen one in the Melbourne Zoo, but not in the wild. We had also seen many a kangaroo, but we hadn't eaten one yet. Dorthy and Amee (the Wycliffe translators) had promised to cook it for us if we got one. Borrowing the Howells' car, Bob, Rogar, and I headed out across the Gibson Desert.

The Region Beyond

It was a typical winter's day in Western Australia. The sky was clear and the sun was hot. I remember cutting off two pairs of pants shortly after I got to Warburton so I would have some shorts to wear. The weather was better than anything we got in Maine in the summer! We hadn't driven far from Warburton when we came upon our first wild kangaroo. Rogar had an old 22 rifle, but he was a very poor shot. I recall chasing that first kangaroo over a small hill as Rogar periodically stopped to shoot, but he always missed. It was after that first encounter we discovered why he had missed: the front sights on the gun were missing! If we got any kangaroo meat, it would be by the grace of God.

The journey continued around sand dunes and through small gaps in mountain (more like hills) ranges scattered along the road. We did run into one couple in a camper traveling through to Alice Springs, but that was the only human life we saw. Rogar showed us where his people found water and game and bushes (no trees in that part of the desert) whose seeds could be eaten. And just before we arrived at the foot of the Blackstone Ranges, Rogar got lucky—or the Lord intervened—and he shot a medium-size kangaroo. We loaded it on the top of the roof of the car and moved on to the place they called Blackstone.

It was afternoon before we arrived at the sign post for Blackstone. One of my prized pictures is of Rogar and me standing under the road sign at Blackstone. The picture that Bob took was of a 12-foot post with five signs nailed to it. B-L-A-C-K-S-T-O-N-E was at the top and below was Warburton—134 miles, Kalgoorlie—723 miles, Docker River—126 miles, and Alice Springs—523 miles. We had reached the heart of the Gibson Desert! We had reached the end of the road for us. Bob and I now knew the boundary of 'our region beyond'!

37

The Word of God

Hebrews 4:12: "For the word of God is quick, and powerful, and sharper than any two-edged sword, piercing even to the dividing asunder of soul and spirit, and of the joints and marrow, and is a discerner of the thoughts and intents of the heart."

ANOTHER ONE OF THE dates that stand out in my Australia adventure is July 16, 1972. The day after Bob, Rogar, and I returned from our Blackstone sightseeing tour with kangaroo in hand (Dorthy and Amee were as good as their word, so Bob and I did get to sample kangaroo, and it wasn't deer steak or moose meat, but it was good!), we sat in on a very special dedication service.

For years, the translators of UFM and Wycliffe had been laboring to translate the Word of God into the Wongi dialect. During the Sunday morning service at the Aboriginal Church at Warburton, Dorthy and Amee presented to the head elder of the tribe a copy of the book of Genesis in Pitjantjara. I remember recognizing the melody to the Doxology as the prayer of dedication was finished:

Palyanyku watjanmalatju.

Mamalu nyangka Katjalu

The Region Beyond

> Kuuti Palyalu nintinu
>
> Pininyalampa palyatu.
>
> Palyanku watjanmalatju.
>
> Yilkaringkatja pinilu
>
> Pananagkatjalutarayu
>
> Palyanyku watjanma titu.

As I pondered the privilege Bob and I had to witness another book of the Bible (the New Testament had been completed) being turned over to the natives of Western Australia, I reflected on the meaning of the verse printed above. To think that the Word of God was now being heard and understood in a language that didn't even have a written alphabet! Dorthy and Amee had moved in among the people a decade before and had to learn a new dialect, write a readable language, then turn around and teach this people how to read their own language!

While at Warburton, I got a better understanding of the importance of speaking the language of the people. It was also there that I realized I have a hard time learning languages. Dorthy and Amee gave us private lessons during our time there, and it was through them I learned another important requirement of being a missionary to the Aborigines: the ability to learn a very difficult language. It was another one of many skills I didn't possess. Day by day and event by event, the Good Lord was showing me He had not gifted me to be a pioneer missionary.

As I finish this chapter, I have just completed a study and PowerPoint on How We Got Our Bible? One of the aspects of that study was how the Bible has spread throughout the world. In my research, I got on the Wycliffe Translators website and discovered the progress of getting the Bible into the common languages of the world. I discovered these interesting facts:

> There are about 6809 different languages and dialects known in the world today. (All I could think was when

The Word of God

God confused the languages at Babel He did a good job of it-Genesis 11:9.)

By 1800 only 57 people groups had the Bible in their own language, but by 1900 the number had risen to 537. Over the next eighty years (until 1980) that number had grown to 1800. By 2000 that number had reached 2322. In 2003 the statistics were like this: 2322 with some part of the Bible in their native tongue, 2843 still without the written Word, and 1634 translations in progress. There is only about 340 million of the world's population of 7 billion that don't have the Word. I feel we are getting close to a little recognized prophecy of Christ:

> "And this Gospel of the kingdom shall be preached in all the world for a witness unto all nations; AND THEN SHALL THE END COME!" (Matthew 24:14)

I still count it as a privilege the day I was there when a small piece of that prophecy was fulfilled in the Gibson Desert.

38

Rendezvous in Warburton

Mark 5:19: "Go home to thy friends, and tell them how great things the Lord hath done for thee, and hath had compassion on thee."

THE LAUNDRY AND SHOWER building was almost done, and there were a few projects in Cosmo Newbery needing my attention before we headed back across the Nullarbor Plain. As my days in Warburton came to an end, my dear Lord began to speak to me in His famous still, small voice (I Kings 19:12). It wasn't one event or message or conversation with one of the missionaries at Warburton, or even a talk with my cousin Bob. It was that inner tugging of the Spirit of God that brought me to the conclusion I didn't want to face. I wanted to come back to Australia; I wanted to be a missionary on a foreign field; but my Boss was saying, "Go back home!"

It was as hard for me to face the truth as for the demon-possessed man of the Gadarenes (Mark 5:2). After receiving a marvelous cleansing, the man "prayed him that he might be with him. Howbeit Jesus suffered him not, but saith unto him . . . (See scripture above)" (Mark 5:18–19). And as they say, "the rest is history." The man wanted to minister afar, but Jesus told him to "go home." There on a small plateau in the heart of the Gibson Desert, I heard the voice of God say to my soul and my servant's spirit, "Go home to New England and serve me there." I resisted the voice, as Elijah did at first, but how can a mere mortal debate very long with God? It is His work and His plan and His will that must and will be fulfilled in the end. The demonic man wanted to get on the ship with Jesus and follow Him across the Sea of Galilee, and I wanted to again cross the wide Pacific to help reach the children I had learned to love at Warburton. But my Boss was saying:

"Not here, not now, not them!"

As I reflect back on that crossroads in Warburton, I see clearly that God was right. I know now, even more than I knew then, that I was not equipped to be an Australian missionary. My spiritual gifts are in other areas, and neither me not my wife would have survived in the place they call Warburton. If there is one note of joy and understanding after 40 years, it is that part of me—the adventurous missionary part of me—is alive and well in my daughter, Marnie. Marnie has never been to Australia, but she has made two trips to Africa, two trips to India, and one trip to Europe (Nigeria in 1997, Togo in 2001, Slovakia in 2003, India in 2007, 2008). And who knows where she will end up after her studies at Dallas Theological Seminary. I can also report that the adventurous spirit that took me to Australia in 1972 is still alive in me, but my heart's desire has changed from Australia to India!

Does my heart still hurt because of the Lord's choice for me? Yes, it does. But if I have learned anything about my God's choices, it is that 'Father knows best!'

39

They Returned Again

Acts 14:21: "And when they had preached the gospel to that city, and had taught many, they returned again to Lystra, and to Iconium, and Antioch."

ON JULY 23, 1972, I began my long journey back to the United States. Like with Paul and Barnabas at the end of their first missionary trip, there is always a point in which you reach the end of the line. For the first missionary team, it was Derbe (Acts 14:20); for Bob and me, it was Warburton. We had ministered for nearly a month in the world's most remote mission station, and it was time to revisit the Australian saints who had gotten us to Warburton. For Paul and Barnabas it was Lystra, Iconium, and Antioch; for Bob and me, it was Cosmo Newbery, Mount Margaret, and Kalgoorlie.

As with my trip into Warburton, I headed back to Cosmo Newbery alone. Bob would stay in Warburton a few more days to finish up some projects while I returned to Cosmo to help the Cotterills with a few projects around the sheep and cattle station. Once again I rode Kevin Ewing's big rig out of the desert. We left Warburton at 6 in the evening and arrived at Cosmo Newbery around 10 the next morning. It was another beautiful night following the Southern Cross through the sand dunes and rocky

They Returned Again

ridges, and I was given the added thrill of driving most of the way myself. Kevin and I also saw a big, old turkey—a rare sight and the only sign of life we saw in the 300-mile trip! We arrived at the sheep station on Sunday just in time for services.

My first adventure back at Cosmo Newbery was an inspection trip to visit a few of the nearly two dozen windmills on the ranch. They must be checked regularly, for if they are not working, the cattle and sheep will have no water. I was given a 17-year-old Aboriginal boy as a guide, and off we went. We would be spending at least one night in the bush, so we had to take supplies. After inspecting the windmills, and before returning to the station, we would finish fixing one of the many huts that served as shelters during round-ups. I had started the project before I went to Warburton, and I was determined to finish it before I had to head home.

Any trip into the bush is an adventure, but this one I still remember after 40 years. We had four flat tires before we got to the first windmill. Spare tires and patching kits got us through. We also encountered nearly 50 kangaroos (they like the water too). The two projects eventually took us a day and a half, and I took the opportunity to witness to my newest Aboriginal friend. What I did was nothing more than what the earliest missionaries did:

> "Confirming the souls of the disciples, and exhorting them to continue in the faith, and that through much tribulation enter into the kingdom of God" (Acts 14:22).

The return was off to a great start!

40

Cold Water

Proverbs 25:25: "As cold waters to a thirsty soul, so is good news from a far country."

As I WAITED FOR Bob to rejoin me at Cosmo Newbery, I continued to do need repairs around the station. According to a letter I wrote my parents and another I wrote to my girlfriend, I was busy. Besides fixing windmills and fixing walls, I also became a bricklayer:

> "Well, just call me bricklayer Blackstone; add another occupation to my resume of firsts. Today we started to brick up a wall on the building I put a new roof on. This morning I got the porch straightened out and worked at making a new post to replace the old set-up. Then this afternoon, I got started on the bricks. It wouldn't be quite so bad if I had Bob around. I have learned one thing about the Aborigines, and that is they are slow workers and don't like to work as a team! And it takes good teamwork to lay bricks. I bet it took us three hours to lay 30 brick. The best thing that happened today was one of the Aboriginal deacons of the church came by to ask me to preach next Sunday!"

Cold Water

I wrote pieces of letters every day, or nearly every day, but I didn't get letters every day. Needless to say, mail in the outback of Western Australia wasn't fast. I remember it took nearly three weeks before our first letters from home caught up with us. In an old letter I wrote to my parents from Cosmo Newbery, I mention that their newly-arrived letter had taken 11 days to get from Perham to Cosmo, and that it wasn't necessary to write again because by the time the letter arrived, Bob and I would already be home!

Besides letters from my parents and my brothers and sisters, I received letters from my girlfriend and her sister and parents. I also said in a letter home:

> "Just got a letter from Virginia Vough saying her summer was going well. She is having a great time in Queensland and doing children's work. She has seen many saved. Praise the Lord."

It was also through these drinks of 'cold water' from home that I was kept up on family news. I was reminded as I re-read those old letters that the summer of '72 was the summer my Grandmother Barton, my mother's mother, moved to the farm from the city (Gramie would live 20 more years). That was also the summer my brother Jay (12 years younger than me) showed how good he was with a baseball. And I learned from Australia that my older sister and her future husband, who would marry shortly after I got back from Australia, had bought their first home. I know these events in the life of the Blackstone family were not earth-shaking, but they were 'water' for me!

It is amazing to me that even after forty years, sips of 'cold water' still generate memories I thought long left in the past. Sometimes when you walk down memory lane you find a cooling stream of water running alongside!

41

Apollos Watered

I Corinthians 3:6: "I have planted, Apollos watered; but God gave the increase."

IN AN OLD LETTER I had written from Cosmo Newbery to my girlfriend during the summer of '72 I said this:

> "Well, guess what it did today? IT RAINED, and did it rain. The first rain I have seen since we left the States. It really came down, so I couldn't put the roof on the house. Instead, I put in a new window and fixed a door, so I got the wash room done. Kevin (the truck driver) came through today also. Bob ought to be back with him tomorrow. Also there was a geologist here from England all day. He is getting some fossil rocks to ship back to Adelaide. Had an interesting time with him and his sidekick, Beven. . . . . Also got the place ready for Bob's arrival. . . . Am going to finish off my sermon. Going to speak on John 3:16: The Bible Story in a Verse. That is simple. Pray I can get it across and the Holy Spirit will work. . . . This will be our last Sunday at Cosmo Newbery. We will spend one Sunday at Mount Margaret and one more in Melbourne, and the next one we will be home in Perham!"

A bit later in the letter, I wrote this:

"Bob left Warburton (learned by two-way radio) at 12 o'clock last night. . . . It rained a little more today, but most of it went by. That might hold up Bob and Kevin a little. Had a good service this morning. I got up at 9 o'clock, and then we had Sunday school at 9:30. Church was at 11 . . . I had the whole service. I even conducted the communion service here. It was great. I am glad I had a chance to do it. It lasted until 12:15. There were about 20 there counting the kids. Last week the Cotterills had a Sunday school picnic for the kids, and 16 showed up. They barbecued steak and sausage with French fries, and of course cake and tea. While they played games with the kids, I washed the dishes."

The longer I stayed in the outback, the more I realized that mission work was teamwork. There was no way one man or one woman or one couple could do it alone. To reach such a people with the Gospel of Christ required not only planters and those who would water, but also those who would plow and harrow and prepare the heart even before the seed could be planted. I saw clearly at Cosmo Newbery that without a team effort, on many fronts, with many gifted saints, the Aboriginal people of the Gibson Desert would never be saved. I am proud to say that for at least a few weeks, I had the privilege of doing some 'watering.' As the rain from heaven watered Cosmo Newbery, I sprinkled the water of John 3:16 on the hearts of its native people!

It was also there that I was able to experience for the first time what it was like to be a pastor. I was beginning to realize that pastoring was what I had been gifted to do. Now I know why I loved so much that Sunday at Cosmo Newbery. The Sunday the Cotterills allowed a young man from Maine to preach to their flock, conduct a communion service for their flock, and minister to their flock. What I have been for nearly forty years was first realized in 'the region beyond'!

42

Spiritual Adversaries

Ephesians 6:12: "For we wrestle not against flesh and blood, but against principalities, against powers, against rulers of the darkness of this world, against spiritual wickedness in high places."

AS I WAITED FOR Bob to rejoin me at Cosmo Newbery, I continued to do odd jobs around the 'superstation' of 1,250,000 acres. The more I stayed with the Cotterills, the more I realized just what it took to be such a missionary. Two noteworthy characteristics could be seen very clearly in their lives: an ability of perseverance (Ephesians 6:18) and a readiness to 'give it a go' regardless of the odds, physically or spiritually speaking!

The life of an Australian rancher/missionary is an unbelievably hard life, yet they overcome every adversity and adversary through tenacity and courage. The outback missionary faces all the common hazards of the average outback rancher: fire and flood (Yes, flash floods. I still have in my possession a picture, sent to me a few years after Bob and I visited Mount Margaret Station, of Mr. Lanham carrying Mrs. Lanham on his shoulders through knee-deep water. The picture was taken at a spot that I knew well so that I could understand and compare the situation then to when I walked through that same spot. It was bone-dry when Bob and I walked the dusty Wadi, and later was a raging stream!), drought and pestilence. No part of Western Australia is ever free of those four things; their effect is merely a matter of degree. In the outback, like at Cosmo Newbery, the scourge of these conditions is accepted as an inescapable factor of living in such a land. But the missionary/rancher must also factor in the spiritual adversaries as well.

Bob and I soon learned after traveling into the Gibson Desert that we had crossed into the Devil's country. The Devil and his demons were worshipped there more than the Lord. We felt spiritual oppression almost immediately like we had never experienced before or since. The land was hostile, but so were the wanderers of the land. Not everybody accepted with open arms the attempt of UAM to help. We saw no physical attacks, but spiritual attacks were constant both at Warburton and Cosmo Newbery. These two places were on the front lines. Tiredness, despite our youthful ages, quickly overcame Bob and me. The missionaries explained to us the importance of both physical and spiritual rest. I experienced firsthand the importance of spiritual armor and the need to put it on (Ephesians 6:11) daily. It was in the Gibson Desert that I learned the only way to stand and withstand 'spiritual wickedness in high places' was to "be strong in the Lord, and in the power of His might" (Ephesians 6:10). The Devil was good, but God's men and women were better!

43

Trouble in Warburton

Ephesians 6:16: "Above all, taking the shield of faith, wherewith ye shall be able to quench all the fiery darts of the wicked."

WHEN BOB FINALLY CAUGHT up with me at Cosmo Newbery, what stories he had to tell!

First, Bob was happy to report that the 28-foot-long by 14-foot-wide by 7-foot-tall shower and laundry room was done, including the hot water system—the last part of the project. Bob had stayed behind to finish the work, including a double barrel, wood-fired heating plant. In my collection of pictures, I have one of Bob sitting on the two barrels. The twin barrels were placed on a rock fireplace, and the water was tapped into the drums both on the top and bottom. Cold water was piped into the top, and the hot water was piped out of the bottom. It was a simple system, but it gave all the hot water that was needed. I know it worked because at the cabin Bob and I stayed in at Cosmo there was a single barrel. I remember coming home after a hard day's work and taking a shower after I built a fire under the barrel. A few minutes later, I had all the hot water I wanted! It was always amazing to me just how adaptable these people were.

Second, Bob could not wait to tell me about the war that had taken place in Warburton on his last day there. A bit of history first: like with our Native Americans, when the British invaded the homelands of the Aborigines, they brought with them disease and drink. Diseases not found in Aboriginal society before brought death to many, but the worse curse was alcohol. I remember one night at Cosmo when Mr. Cotterill had to deal with a couple of men that returned drunk from Laverton. There was no drink on the stations, but in the nearby towns there was plenty to be found. When an Aborigine gets drunk, he can become very dangerous, and many had died in the fights that followed. If someone died at the hand of another, then revenge was in order from the family of the dead man. Feuds were common, and at any moment a major fight could break out over a wrong of any kind. I never wrote in my letter to my girlfriend what the war was over, but Bob witnessed a major confrontation the day he drove out of Warburton.

The very long spears I described in an earlier chapter were used against each other, and a number of men were wounded and had to be treated by the missionaries. Nobody died, but the event reminded me of the verse printed above. Unless we keep our shield high and our sword unsheathed, our enemy the Devil will get his 'fiery darts' through and we too will be wounded. I have spent the bulk of my 40 years in the pastorate helping wounded saints recover. Whether on the dusty plateau of Warburton, or the well-watered plains of America, a war is going on, and we are the Devil's target. Let us never forget:

> "Be sober, be vigilant; because your adversary the devil, as a roaring lion, walketh about, seeking whom he may devour." (I Peter 5:8)

44

A Strange People of a Strange Land

Jeremiah 35:7: "...that ye may live many days in the land where ye be strangers."

As Bob and I packed our bags and our Australian souvenirs for the long trip home, we got one final lesson about the people group known as 'The Gibson Desert Aborigines.' We had spent our summer with an interesting group of people and had met an even more amazing group of missionaries laboring among these spiritually needy people.

Bob and I had been introduced to Australian Aboriginal society through the experiences of the missionaries called by God to reach this particular people group. Our new Australian friends were up against thousands of years of tribal traditions and a belief in 'dreamtime.' When I came home, I found this eye-opening definition of 'dreamtime':

> "The complex root of Aboriginal faith is 'dreamtime,' a timeless age before the historic past but continuing now. In the 'dreamtime' totemic beings, such as the opossum, the kangaroo, and the water snake, traveled across the desert, leaving their influence in sacred places, still to influence the lives of people today. The tracks taken by the dreamtime beings cross and re-cross in a web over

the desert . . . cult-lodges, consisting of men who believe themselves to be descended in the male line from the same 'dreamtime' beings, still haunt the land today!"

While Bob and I were at Warburton, we could hear from the Howells' home the 'sacred dances' and 'sacred songs' being sung. We were never allowed to watch these 'satanic' ceremonies, but we saw enormous bonfires on the plains below Warburton. We heard firsthand how difficult it was for an Aborigine to break free from these traditions. It was common for an Aboriginal man to take more than one wife, and the difficulty that results when salvation takes place. We did visit the corrugated iron shacks of the Aborigines and saw for ourselves the terrible poverty in which they lived. Bob and I were there when the impact of Westernized society on primitive man was both seen and not seen. Nakedness was no concern to these people, as Bob and I experienced during a few embarrassing moments, but for the most part clothing was the norm. (Probably the funniest clothing story of the trip was when Bob and I were putting on the roof of the shower and laundry building and an Aboriginal man walked by in a raccoon (or at least that is what it looked like to us) coat. It was an afternoon well into the 90's, but the man was dressed for a January in Maine! It was also the closest we got to actual conflict, when the man approached us thinking we were laughing at him. One of the missionaries soon had him on his way.)

According to my last letter to my girlfriend, the final thing Bob and I did for the Aborigines was give them a dead kangaroo we had found caught in a fence. Bob cut the tip of the tail off as a souvenir, but the people of Cosmo Newbery were happy with our present. We were leaving the 'strange land' of a 'strange people,' or was it we who were strangers there?

I have often pondered years since how the people of the Warburton Range saw Bob and me. Two young men building strange things in shorts and tie-shirts in the middle of winter: wearing a fur coat was normal, wearing no coat was strange! To them we had come from a distant land, it might have well been

Mars in their eyes. We talked with an unknown tongue and we told them of a story of a Man from Galilee, another "Stranger" from a strange place!

45

Goodbye to the Gibson Desert

II Corinthians 13:11: "Finally, brethren, farewell."

OUR GOODBYES TO OUR newfound Christian and Aboriginal friends began on the morning of August 3, 1972, when Mr. Cotterill called Warburton on the mission's two-way radio. That early morning radio call allowed Bob and me to say a proper goodbye and heart-felt 'thank you' to the people of Warburton for their wonderful hospitality and marvelous acceptance of two boys from Maine. I was excited about leaving for home, but I was sad to think I might never see these dear saints again this side of heaven: the Howells, Herbert, Lorraine, and Beven, our adopted family in Australia. We stayed with them longer than anybody else in the land down under. (They are also the only individuals with which I remained in contact for many years.) We also said goodbye to the Siggs, Ken and Mary, our co-workers among the Aboriginal children; Amee Glass and Dorthy Hackett, our language teachers and kangaroo cooks. Then there was Phyllis, the lady we had met at the mission hospital at Warburton, and the Perry's, the couple at the mission store that gave us many a wonderful treat during our stay on the Warburton Range Mission Station in Western Australia.

The Region Beyond

At Cosmo Newbery, we said 'goodbye' to Claude and Dora, our second parents in Australia. Our stay with them was only a few days shorter than ours with the Howells. Dora made sure all our clothes were clean before we left, very mother-like. We had to say goodbye to Sockey the dog as well. According to a letter I wrote to Coleen, Bob and I left Cosmo Newbery on a Thursday by riding into Laverton with a friend of one of the public school teachers; I never recorded the name, just one of the many nameless people who helped us on our trip throughout Australia. At Laverton, we stayed for a while and had supper with Kevin Ewing and his dear wife at their home, a chance to say goodbye to the man who took us in and out of the real 'bush,' and gave me two unforgettable experiences under the Australian sky!

Later that evening, Charlie Lanham picked us up and drove us back to Mount Margaret Mission Station, where we stayed for a couple of days. While there, we said our goodbyes and continued our summer's work. Instead of constructing something, we did some deconstructing. An old building on the station had to come down, so Bob and I and a few Aboriginal boys knocked it down and picked up the pieces to burn. In the rubble, I found an old skeleton key that I have today as a souvenir of our last work project in Australia. Before our final goodbye to the Lanhams, they took us to explore an old gold mine. Like at Kalgoorlie, we found no earthly gold but left the Gibson Desert with a mind full of golden memories that have remained untarnished all these years!

46

Detour

Jeremiah 10:23: "O Lord, I know that the way of man is not in himself; it is not in man that walketh to direct his steps."

WHEN BOB AND I left Mount Margaret, we thought we were headed for Kalgoorlie and the Trans-Australian train. We did not know it then, but our Lord had one final detour for His servants from Maine!

Who among us hasn't been driving down a pleasant roadway when we come across a 'Detour' sign? That loathsome instruction forces us away from our planned route of travel. More often than not, we have to turn abruptly onto some dirty side road that leads us over a very rough terrain. Unlike our super-smooth interstate highway, the detour is full of curves, bumps, and hills. We grumble as we have to slow down and growl because of all the time we are losing. As for me, I like detours! Often those drab trails have led me through colorful meadows and blossoming orchards I would have missed if I hadn't been detoured; open country, away from the rushing traffic and busy crowds; and man-made signs that blight God's wonderful creation. There have been times I wished the detour would not end!

Life itself has detours. An old preacher once said:

> "We set out upon the highway of some fixed course we have chosen and mapped and planned for ourselves. Then one day around some sudden bend of the road, we find our thoroughfare blocked and the side road in its place. Businesses crash, health fails, dear ones die, disaster comes; we must abandon the way we meant to go and try some shabby trail of shattered dreams, fallen hopes, and breaking hearts. We start our wearily upon it and find, to our surprise, that it leads to treasures and beauty we never would have found elsewhere!"

When John Bunyan was detoured through Bedford Prison, he found *Pilgrim's Progress*. When Stanley was detoured through Africa, he found Livingstone. When Paul ran into the Damascus detour (Acts 9:3), he was led down glorious roads of service he never would have traveled, if not for that detour. So it will be with us—Australia was such a detour for me!

At first, we are unsure of its virtue over the main road we travel, but the farther we follow this slow road, the more we are sure it is the better road. Unlike the road we were on before, this detour can't be traveled quickly. There is time to stop and look around and see the world around us. On the super highway of self-will, the scenery was nothing but a blur. Now the road is clear and the way is lined with wonderful blessings we would have missed if we hadn't taken God's detour! We must believe that despite the detour, God's side roads in life do hold their own compensations. Whether a crushing detour that takes you from a rosy road to a drab driveway of infirmity, or a running path of success to plodding along a narrow lane with one misfortune after another, when the journey is over and we look back on this burdensome boulevard, we will conclude with Paul:

"I have finished my course" (II Timothy 4:7)

Detours and all! Just like the detour Bob and I experienced as we headed out of the Gibson Desert.

47

From Mount Margaret to Cundeelee

Romans 4:12: "...who also walk in the steps of that faith...?"

BOB AND I LEFT Mount Margaret Mission Station on August 6, 1972 (Coleen's and my 37-month anniversary going steady) in the car of our old friend, Mr. Brown, the native welfare officer who had helped us before. He was traveling from Laverton, where he had his home and headquarters, to Kalgoorlie on business. Unlike our fly-in trip, we drove the five hours to Kalgoorlie, where we had our final goodbye with Wilf and Beth Douglas. They were as kind and helpful to us the second time around as they had been the first time we showed up at their door. It was then we found out we would not be catching the train at Kalgoorlie; other plans had been made for the two lads from America.

We stayed the night of the 6th with the Douglas' at their home in Kalgoorlie, and on the 7th we were off again. Our destination was the Australia Evangelical Mission Station at Cundeelee. Despite its name, it wasn't an Australian mission, but an organization founded in Canada. UAM thought it might be nice for Bob and me to see another style of mission. We were driven to the out-of-the-way station, over 150 miles east of Kalgoorlie and 20 miles north of the Trans-Australian Railroad Line at Zanthus, by a friend of the Douglas', Mr. Wentworth. It was

The Region Beyond

on that trip Bob and I experienced our first emu in the wild. The huge bird ran in front of the car for a few miles (much like the moose in Maine like to do).

The trip into Cundeelee was similar to our trips into Leonora and Mount Margaret, except we saw a lot more trees. We aren't talking about big trees, but compared to the small shrubs and bushes of the Gibson Desert, it was as if we were driving through forest land. It was a pleasant ride, and as before, we were greeted like long lost friends by the missionaries at the Cundeelee Mission. It was also at the Cundeelee station that we met our first Americans since our God-ordained meeting with Mr. Garlock in Melbourne.

We had two wonderful days with the missionaries of the Australian Evangelical Mission at Cundeelee, before we were to pick up the Trans-Australian Train on August 9 at Zanthus. At Cundeelee we met the Days, a young American family working for the Lord in Western Australia. We also got to know Mr. Hislop, a man who had paid the ultimate price for his service in a harsh and hostile land: his wife had just given her life in the Lord's service. We also met Mr. Davidson, a veteran missionary who had spent the bulk of his life ministering in China and Japan and who had retired to minister to the Aborigines of Cundeelee. Another American couple that touched our hearts was the Petersons. Mr. Peterson was the station mechanic. Though these individuals and families only touched our lives for less than 48 hours, I say today, forty years later, that their walk and work of faith was a testimony to their love of our Savior!

I often wonder where they all are now. Most of the elderly saints not doubt are in heaven, but what of the others. Are they still in Cundeelee or another Cundeelee trying to reach the unreached with the Gospel of Christ? As I start my 21st year in my Cundeelee (Ellsworth) I am reminded that I too have learned perseverance!

48

Life's Railway to Heaven

Matthew 7:21: "Not every one that saith unto me, Lord, Lord, shall enter into the kingdom of heaven; but he that doeth the will of my Father which is in heaven."

ON THE MORNING OF August 9, 1972, my cousin and I were driven down to Zanthus to catch a train east. When I say 'catch,' I mean catch. Because our return tickets were stamped from Kalgoorlie to Melbourne, we were not expected in Zanthus. Zanthus was just a stop along the way, and if there were no expected passengers, the train just rolled through town. I have a picture of Bob literally flagging down the Trans-Australian Train at Zanthus. Because they were not expecting us, we literally had to run along the track after the train while trying to convince the conductor in the last car we had tickets for the trip! It was the only time in Western Australia I thought we might be stranded in the Nullarbor Plain. Throwing our bags on board and jumping on a moving train, Bob and I eventually persuaded the conductor we were supposed to be on the train. It was a final adventure in the wilds of Western Australia that taught me the importance of getting 'on the train.'

Interestingly, my future father-in-law, Stacy Meister, was a railroad conductor. When I got to know him a little better, he taught me one of his favorite hymns, *Life's Railway to Heaven*. It goes like this:

> "Life is like a mountain railroad (or a plains railroad!), with an Engineer that's brave; we must make the run successful from the cradle to the grave. Watch the curves, the fills, the tunnels, never falter, never quail; keep your hand upon the throttle and your eye upon the rail. You will roll up grades of trial, you will cross the bridge of strife; see that Christ is your conductor on this lightening train of life; always mindful of obstruction, do your duty, never fail; keep your hand upon the throttle, and your eye upon the rail. You will often find obstructions, look for storms and wind and rain; on a fill or curve or trestle they will almost ditch your train; put your trust alone in Jesus, never falter, never fail; keep your hand upon the throttle, and your eye upon the rail. As you roll across the trestle spanning Jordan's swelling tide, you behold the Union Depot into which your train will glide; there you'll meet the Superintendent, God the Father, God the Son; with the hearty, joyous plaudit, 'Weary pilgrim, welcome home!' Blessed Savior, Thou wilt guide us, till we reach that blissful shore, where the angels wait to join us in Thy praise forever more!"

It was our ticket that finally convinced the Conductor and got Bob and me on that Trans-Australian Train, and it will be the ticket stamped with Jesus' name (Acts 4:12) that will get you on the heaven-bound train of Christ!

49

Walter F. Betts

Zechariah 4:6: "...Not by might, nor by power, but by my Spirit, saith the Lord of hosts."

As Bob and I rolled back into Melbourne after nearly two months in the outback of Australia, we returned as 'heroes' to our Australia home church, The People's Church in Kew. We had done what nobody in that church had ever done. Everyone was excited to hear of our spiritual adventures, and for a couple of days, we were the talk of the church. In the background of all this excitement was an elderly man of 80 years, Walter F. Betts. It was our privilege to get to know this famous Australian before we left for America.

Born in 1892, the fifth of six children, Walter Betts was the son of a wheat farmer. Brought up in the Methodist Church, Walter was converted at the age of 18. It wasn't until he met Rev. J.H. Cain that his spiritual life dramatically changed. Cain's first question to the young Betts was, "Any fish in the net?" "Fish?" asked Walter. "I wasn't fishing!" It took a couple of weeks for the meaning of the question to sink in, but when it did, Walter F. Betts began to walk on a path that would make him one of the greatest soul winners in Australian Church history.

For the next 37 years, Walter Betts traveled through nearly every community, both great and small, on the east coast of Australia. Everywhere he went, revival broke out and hundreds and hundreds were brought into the Kingdom. Dying churches were built up again, and new churches were organized. In 1954, three years after my birth, Walter Betts resigned from the Methodist Church because of the growing modernism movement. He started pastoring the Melbourne People's Church of Kew. When Bob and I met this godly man, he had just turned 80. He was as sharp as ever and still preaching. His life's verse is printed above, and if my memory serves me well, those were the first words out of his mouth when we met him. He had been away preaching during our first stay in Melbourne.

Walter had a colorful way of saying things, and in a biography written by Dallas Clarnette, I found these sayings worth repeating:

"We need Pauline Christians, not poor lean Christians."

"Jesus is the joy filler not a joy killer."

"I can fellowship with anyone who is right on the Book and the Blood."

"In churches today, we hear much about the Home Mission and the Overseas Mission, but more should be said about submission."

"A man is not what he thinks he is, but what a man thinks! He is."

"Four are always present: the Father, the Son, the Holy Spirit, and the Devil to p-r-e-y!"

To this day I still remember the encouragement this saint of God gave to me in our Lord's work. He must be listed with the many that helped me see my true calling!

50

The Statue of Liberty

Galatians 5:1: "Stand fast therefore in the liberty wherewith Christ hath made us free ..."

ON AUGUST 13, 1972, our new Melbourne friends put us on a plane bound for Sydney. In Sydney, we again met up with Virginia, and then on a very windy and cold August day, we boarded a plane for the Fiji Islands. Unlike our trip to Australia, our return flight would take us through this South Pacific paradise. We arrived to fuel up for our long flight to Hawaii. It was warm and pleasant despite arriving in the dark. We saw little of the island before we boarded our trans-oceanic flight. Because we had to re-cross the International Dateline, August 13 never seemed to end. Despite leaving Fiji late in the day, by the time we arrived in the States, it was still August 13. I remembered then the biblical story of Joshua:

> "So the sun stood still in the midst of the heaven, and hasted not to go down about a whole day" (Joshua 10:13).

We changed flights in LA and sent Virginia home on a different plane. Bob and I flew across the country on a 747, our first, and as we flew into New York, we caught a glimpse of the Statue of Liberty. It was then I really knew I was home. As I ponder those last few minutes of that summer missionary trip, the words and music of Neil Enloe, written just a couple of summers after I returned to America, flood my mind:

> "In New York harbor stands a lady, with a torch raised to the sky; and all who see her, know she stands for Liberty for you and me. I'm so proud to be called an American, to be named with the brave and the free; I will honor our flag, and our trust in God, and the Statue of Liberty!"

"On lonely Golgotha stood a cross, with my Lord raised to the sky; and all who kneel there live forever as all the saved can testify. I'm so glad to be called a Christian, to be named with the ransomed and whole; as the statue liberates the citizen, so the Cross liberates the soul. Oh, the cross is my Statue of Liberty; it was there that my soul was set free; unashamed I'll proclaim that a rugged cross is my Statue of Liberty!"

It was John the Apostle who proclaimed these words of Christ:

> "If ye continue in my word, then ye are my disciples indeed; and ye shall know the truth, and the truth shall make you free . . . If the Son therefore shall make you free, ye shall be free indeed" (John 8:31–32, 36).

As Bob and I flew home from New York by way of Boston, it was that image of the Statue of Liberty that symbolized my homecoming, and the beginning of a new ministry to my own people. I had discovered in Australia that I was to be a missionary to America, not a missionary to Australia!

Postlude

Genesis 24:27: "...I being in the way, the Lord led me..."

YOU MUST HAVE FIGURED out by now that Bob and I made it home again. Before the longest day of my life was over, my cousin and I had traveled from Australia back to our home in Northern Maine. To conclude the story, I thought I would share with you just what the Lord did in my life after He redirected my focus and my future while in Warburton.

Both Bob and I returned to Bob Jones University a few weeks after arriving home from Australia: Bob to his junior year and me to my senior year. I graduated with a Bachelor of Arts in Bible and a minor in History on May 30, 1973. Three weeks later, I married the girlfriend I mentioned, Coleen. The date was June 21, 1973, and Bob was my best man. (Two days before, on June 19, I was the best man at his wedding; he came back from his honeymoon to be my best man—what a guy!) Within two weeks of our marriage, Coleen and I started a new church under the church planting program of Bob Jones University. The Pembroke Bible Fellowship was a direct result of God's clear message to my heart at Warburton to go home!

Over the next five years, Coleen and I poured our hearts and talents into this new work. We moved four times in five years, but were never able to establish the church in a central location. Besides pastoring the church, I held down another full-time job. Within five years, I was physically exhausted. God told me I had to make a choice, so I left our first church to seek a full-time position in an established church. This decision took

Coleen and me and our son, Scott (he was seven months old at the time), north to Maine. I began my first full-time pastorate at Calvary Baptist Church in Westfield, Maine, in 1979. This small country church was our home for the next seven and a half years. In many respects, it was our toughest ministry, even though we made a number of cherished friends who are friends to this day. It was also the place the Lord took a child home to glory and gave us the apple of our eye: our daughter.

In 1986, I felt called to pastor my home church but was rejected by the church itself. The Lord opened up a church on an island off the Downeast Coast of Maine, both to fulfill our calling and heal our pastoral hearts. The Washington Street Baptist Church became our home for five years. It was during that stay that the Lord opened my heart to the joy of writing. The people at Eastport also restored my love for pastoring, and I haven't looked back since. The healing my family and I received from the sweet saints on that Maine Island will forever be remembered by me and mine!

In 1991, I was called to the church I still pastor, Emmanuel Baptist Church of Ellsworth, Maine. This church has become 'home' to my wife and children. Through the high school and college years, we have stayed our ground to bring stability to the two main individuals the Good Lord gave us to bring up in his love and grace. Today Scott is a specialist in the United States Army stationed at Fort Bragg in North Carolina (Scott has already done tours of service in Iraq and Afghanistan). Today Marnie is finishing up a Master's program at Dallas Theological Seminary with a desire to be a college professor.

The Lord has led me faithfully, and as with Eliezer of old, I say:

"I being in the way, the Lord has led me" (Genesis 24:27).

Granted, part of 'the way' was a side trip to Australia, but it is on those side trips we learn a lot about ourselves and our Savior. Recently, I read this is a devotional book by Vance Havner:

Postlude

"God lays aside His co-workers as the carpenter his tools. Some are castaways, disapproved. Some are old and spent. A preacher who once swayed multitudes fades out in seclusion. We have our day and some finish early, dying in full bloom. All that matters is that the work goes on, the building goes up. We are not mere pawns on a chessboard, for God is our Father, but we serve our generation by the will of God and then fall asleep and are laid with our fathers. The planters and builders come and go and are nothing—only God is anything and everything!"

If I learned anything from my time in Australia, it was the truth Havner speaks about. I am but a tool in the hand of God (Romans 6:13). I am but an instrument to be used by Him at His choosing. I am but a vessel (II Timothy 2:20) in God's 'great house,' and though I desired to be a golden vessel to serve Him afar, He chose me to be an 'earthen vessel' to serve Him in the back room of His 'great house!' I didn't get what I wanted, but He did, and I have done my best to be a "vessel unto honor, sanctified, and meet for the master's use, prepared unto every good work" (II Timothy 2:21). I close with a chorus I learned at a summer camp in Canada many years ago, a simple message was written by Alfred B. Smith:

> "Filled to overflowing, hearts aglow and showing Christ to those who do not know Him; sanctified and holy, yielded to Him only, vessels for the master's use. O make my life a blessing, Lord, may it stand thy testing, Lord!"

After 40 years, this is still my song and supplication!
—Barry Blackstone
June 7, 2012

Postscript: Bob graduated BJU in 1974. He and his wife, Bonnie, returned to farm and raise two children in our home state of Maine. After 20 years of being a potato farmer and lay preacher, Bob took a job with a large chemical company and pastored a small country church. After 30 years, he has resigned his position and became the executive pastor of the largest church in our home country. After 40 years Bob is now a truck driver traveling all over the eastern United States while doing some laying preaching on the side. As for Virginia, we lost contact shortly after graduation. I occasionally hear from Australia, and still dream of the day I might return and see the changes after forty years!

www.ingramcontent.com/pod-product-compliance
Lightning Source LLC
Chambersburg PA
CBHW070923160426
43193CB00011B/1566